THE OEDIPUS COMPLEX

A PHILOSOPHICAL STUDY

SEYMOUR KEITLEN

"The Oedipus Complex: A Philosophical Study," by Seymour Keitlen. ISBN 1-58939-510-7.

Published 2003 by Virtualbookworm.com Publishing Inc., P.O. Box 9949, College Station, TX, 77842, US. ©2003 Seymour Keitlen. All rights reserved. No part of this publication may be reproduced, stored in a retrieval system, or transmitted in any form or by any means, electronic, mechanical, recording or otherwise, without the prior written permission of Seymour Keitlen.

Manufactured in the United States of America.

CONTENTS

I. INTRODUCTION

This small book presents a study of the Oedipus complex in the work of Sigmund Freud, creator of psychoanalysis.

A problem immediately presents itself, however, in discussing a psychoanalytic idea such as this one. The problem is that forces of resistance spring up to resist or altogether reject the idea. And, there are very good reasons for this reaction.

The idea refers to events that take place in the unconscious mind. Since these events are not accessible to the reader's conscious mind, it would be foolhardy and sanguine to expect the reader to accept something that he cannot relate to his own experiences or memories.

The complex is unconscious because its conscious perception would produce painful feelings of anxiety and guilt. Resistant, protective barriers are therefore present in everyone. These barriers can be lifted, nonetheless, by psychoanalytic methods, which allow the individual to obtain knowledge of unconscious Oedipal conflicts, if and when this is needed.

There are, nevertheless, some individuals who have an unusual awareness of, and contact with, the unconscious mind, without the benefit of psychoanalysis. They have been able to understand and use their knowledge, along with those who acquired their knowledge through therapy.

The eighteenth century encyclopedist, Diderot, recognized the incestuous and parricidal wishes that are present in children, but he never developed the idea. Friedrich Nietzsche described many psychoanalytic insights long before the development of psychoanalysis.

A charming example is the short story by Frank O'Connor, called "My Oedipus Complex," in which the author humorously describes what can easily be observed of the complex in everyday life. (See <u>The Stories of Frank O'Connor</u>, Alfred A. Knopf. Inc. N.Y., 1950.)

This study, accordingly, can hardly lead to emotional acceptance of, or conviction of, the reality of the Oedipus complex. It is a study that, paradoxically, a part of every reader's mind will want to reject or at the very least to misunderstand. The ideas related to the Oedipus complex are all simple psychological ideas. However, because so much emotion is attached to them they often produce "emotional stupidity," a phrase coined by Freud to apply to the lack of understanding produced by resistance.

What this work can provide is an intellectual understanding of the idea. Intellectual comprehension is not to be depreciated, nonetheless, since it is necessary before emotional, convincing acceptance can take place. It remains, however, insufficient and in itself incapable of carrying conviction. Or rather, it carries conviction so long as it is applied to others and not oneself.

The Oedipus complex is a theory about the mental life of the child.

Briefly summarized, it is a theory that postulates that in early childhood, between the ages of two and six, the young child develops two emotional ties to its parents, namely, a purely affectionate tie to the parent of the opposite sex and a hostile tie to the parent of the same sex, taken as a rival.

The term itself was aptly chosen because of the similarity between the child's wishes, to possess one parent and replace the other, and the deeds of Oedipus Rex, the hero of the famous Greek drama of Sophocles.

The word "complex" is used as a convenient term for summing up descriptively all the elements of a very intricate psychological situation. To use a physical analogy, the complex consists of the triangular interrelationships existing between a child and its mother and father; and the perceptions, emotions, and attitudes contained in these relationships.

Although the idea is essentially concerned with the life of the child, its sphere of application extends beyond the confines of child psychology. It can be applied to problems of adult psychology and psychopathology, since adult behavior is greatly decided by events which take place in

3

childhood. Moreover, certain aspects of the history of the human race, morality, and religion have been elucidated by its application to cultural anthropology.

———————

The ideas inherent in the idea appeared very early in the course of Freud's psychoanalytic work. Increasing experience led to recognition of the concept's importance. Freud came to regard the complex as the central experience of the years of childhood and the nuclear complex of the neuroses.

It is somewhat unique because no idea in the domain of depth psychology has stirred so fierce an opposition and such incredulous denials. It was, at one time, the Shibboleth of psychoanalysis.

At the end of his career, he was to make the dramatic statement that: "if psychoanalysis could boast of no other achievement than the discovery of the repressed Oedipus complex, that alone would give it a claim to be counted among the precious new acquisitions of mankind."[1]

There are still many analysts today that would like to diminish its importance, in favor of some idea of their own.

Resistance to the idea never ends.

Freud made his initial discoveries alone, in totally unexplored territory. There were no maps or guides available. The neuroses were truly terra incognita. He was occasionally helped on his way by a hysterical patient who told him to stop his incessant hypnotic commands, to be quiet and listen to her thoughts.

The great French neurologist, Charcot, had just made hysteria a legitimate illness. Although he knew about the sexual causation of neurosis, he never thought to develop or pursue the idea; since he knew the kind of negative reaction this would provoke. The only treatment available for the neuroses at that time was mild electrotherapy and hypnosis. This only resulted in the removal of symptoms that were suggested away temporarily.

In spite of Charcot, the medical community believed that the neuroses were meretricious, degenerate, fabrications of the patient designed to gain attention. Whereas, doctors who treated them were considered fakes and charlatans.

On the road to discovery, he lost his friend and early collaborator, Josef Breur, who succumbed to the heat of transference and counter transference. He was isolated and shunned by the provincial and anti-Semitic Viennese medical community for ten years. His insistence on the sexual basis of the neuroses made him an unpopular figure in hypocritical, licentious Vienna. Vienna during Freud's lifetime was considered the most anti-Semitic of all the great cities of the world. One out of every three births in pre-war Vienna was illegitimate, reflecting its easygoing moral license.

His initial theories sometimes followed mistaken paths. The forces of internal resistance within and external resistant forces without beset him. Martin Heidegger once suggested to Freud that it was his will to power that enabled him to persevere. There was probably some truth to this observation.

———————

There is no such thing as a unique "Oedipus complex."

Rather, there is a complex that develops in childhood and changes during further development to maturity. In addition, Freud's understanding of the complex changed during his research. Consequently, this study is organized on both temporal and developmental lines.

For purposes of clear exposition, his work related to the idea can be divided into three periods. The first period commences with his discovery of the complex in 1897, and it ends with the first appearance of the actual term in his published writings in 1910.

It is characterized by the abandonment of the seduction theory in the etiology of the neuroses and the study of infantile sexuality. It will be recalled that this led to the first formulation of the libido theory and a dynamic conception of the mind. The libido theory complements the concept of the Oedipus complex. It was used in its turn to explain the origin and development of the complex.

The second period extends from the first appearance of the term in his writings to the introduction of an important change in its definition, a change that took place in 1923. The second period is characterized by many applications of the idea. The applications of the idea show its extraordinary power to explain phenomena that had been described before, but never explained at all. It also contains an intriguing bold attempt to explain the origin of the complex along phylogenetic lines.

The third period includes all of Freud's writings that appeared after 1923. It coincides with the formulation of the tripartite structural theory of the mind and the dual instinct theory. It is noteworthy because of an attempt to explain the origin of the complex along ontogenetic lines.

———

From the time of its discovery to the time of his death, Freud changed and revised the theory.

This did not present a problem for professional analysts, who followed the protean changes in recondite books and journals. It did, of course, result in an oversimplified version reaching the public at large. This tended to swell the tide of resistance and misunderstanding.

The multiple versions that are present in Freud's works reflect, accordingly, the evolution of the idea throughout a veritable lifetime of scientific research, extending over approximately half a century.

The various views and theories in these three periods appear confusing not to say conflicting, unless the evolution of the idea is traced chronologically.

When this is done, a consistent, coherent, and cogent theory emerges.

From time to time, Freud reviewed and updated several of his most important theories, e.g., the libido theory. He did not provide a comprehensive review of the theory of the Oedipus complex. Therefore, no single, comprehensive interpretation of the Oedipus complex exists. Different analysts have interpreted it in multiple ways. Many psychiatrists have never understood its significance.

I therefore thought that it would be worthwhile to summarize the evolution of the idea. It is this task that I have set myself in the pages that follow.

However, the best laid plans of mice and men certainly do go astray. And so it was, that when I prepared this essay, I was forced to critically review old entrenched ideas. So, I found that I learned something new. I developed a conception of the significance of the Oedipus complex that differed from Freud's. This new perspective is described in the penultimate section of this study under metapsychological reflections.

II. EARLY HISTORY

Freud's letters to his intellectually gifted friend and confidant, Wilhelm Fliess, enable us to reconstruct the setting of his initial insight into the Oedipus complex. A letter of May 31, 1897, reveals that his analytic work had already shown him that hostile impulses against parents were an integral part of neurosis. These hostile impulses were discovered in the analysis of obsessive ideas, delusions of persecution, and self-reproaches for the death of a parent.

Furthermore, a clue as to the origin of these hostile impulses was provided by the fact that they were directed toward the parent of the same sex: death wishes of sons were directed against their father and death wishes of daughters were directed against their mother.[2]

A complete insight was only attained, however, when Freud realized that the hostile impulses toward one parent were engendered by love for the other.

And, it was his self-analysis, undertaken during the summer and autumn of 1897, which provided the material that made this recognition possible. In a letter dating from this period, October 15, 1897, he wrote that he found love of the mother and jealousy of the father in his self-analysis, and he believed that the conjunction of love for one parent and hatred for the other to be a general phenomenon of early childhood.[3]

A further source of insight and confirmation came from the interpretation of dreams, his most outstanding achievement.

Among typical dreams, he found dreams of the death of persons of whom the dreamer is fond. He believed that the meaning of such dreams, as their content suggests, is a wish that the person in question may die; they embody death wishes against parents.

The Infantile Period

The clue to their meaning is again provided by the observation that the dreams of the death of parents apply with preponderant frequency to the parent who is the same sex as the dreamer: men dream of their father's death and women of their mother's death.

These death wishes date from early childhood, and they are related to the fact that the girl's affection is for her father and a boy's first childish desires are for his mother. Accordingly, the father becomes a disturbing rival to the boy and the mother to the girl; the death wishes are an expression of this rivalry. However, for the child, death merely means absence of a parent, since it has not yet learned the meaning of death in the adult meaning of the word.[4]

The possibility of applying this idea to the elucidation of two literary masterpieces seems to have been immediately evident. In the letter mentioned above, there is a discussion of Oedipus Rex and Shakespeare's Hamlet.

It was the analogy between the wishes of childhood and the deeds of Oedipus, who married his mother and murdered his father, which suggested the name for the complex. The two great crimes of Oedipus, incest and parricide, were conceived to represent wishes that are present in parent-child relationships.

In addition, Freud suggested an explanation for the powerful effect of the play on audiences from ancient times right until the present. The play has a profound power to move because the child's wishful fantasy that it contains was present at one time in everyone. The spectator reacts because the hero vicariously fulfills the wishes of childhood. This provides the Aristotelian catharsis.

In Hamlet, the child's wishful fantasy is not expressed. But, the text of the play offers no reason or motive for Hamlet's inhibitions and hesitation in fulfilling the task of revenge assigned to him. Nor does it provide an explanation for his failure to marry Ophelia.

The explanation lies in the peculiar nature of the task; for he cannot kill the uncle who shows him the repressed wishes of his own childhood realized. His scruples stem from his unconscious sense of guilt.[5]

These two plays illustrate the two general scenarios for the expression of the Oedipus complex. In the first, illustrated by Oedipus Rex, derivatives of Oedipal wishes are expressed in deeds or actions. In the second scenario, exemplified by Hamlet, the derivatives of the complex are revealed by defensive measures against actions producing inhibitions, hesitations, or delays. In the first scenario, the complex is more evident; in the second, the complex is concealed by defensive reactions.

Many scientific discoveries are made after a new method of investigation is found, because the new method of investigation provides new data for theory formation. And so it was with psychoanalysis, that came into being because of the use of free association complemented by free-floating attention. The exploration of the unconscious mind by means of this technique made psychoanalysis possible.

As far as I know, Freud stumbled on to this method somehow by serendipity. There was, of course, a German writer who used this method to write novels. He recommended it as a means of using the unconscious as a fertile and abundant source of material. Freud evidently admired this writer, and he paid homage to him by visiting his grave. He may have used this method, in part, because he was familiar with this author's work. Also, it seems that analysis and interpretation was always part of Freud's personal bent and inclination for many years. Be this as it may, Freud used the method to abandon the use of hypnosis, and psychoanalysis was born.

There are many who deny the existence of the unconscious mind, because they have never used the method or had the method used on them. Those who have never used the method are in the same position as those who denied the existence of bacteria, because they had never looked through the newly discovered microscope of Van Leevanhoek, in Holland.

The detractors of psychoanalysis are quick to point out the neurotic traits in Freud's own personality; and slow to recognize that he literally created the instrument for his own cure.

In retrospect, it is easy to see that Freud's original discoveries, were the result of intuitive psychological insights. Although, psychoanalysis does not use the experimental method of the physical sciences, it is still an empirical science. Comparable to Astronomy, which does not use the experimental method either, but employs observation and measurement. Initial hypotheses are checked by empirical data derived from the treatment of patients. It is exceptional in that its treatment method is also a research method.

It is noteworthy that Albert Einstein related that all his original insights concerning the nature of the physical world were derived from intuitive insights, which were only confirmed later by measurements and experiments, (cf. Jeremy Bernstein, EINSTEIN).

The same thing is also true for Mendel, the founder of modern genetics, who new in advance how the flowers would grow in his garden before he counted them.

In summary then, Freud's initial discovery of the Oedipus complex was derived from three sources: his study and treatment of the neuroses, his intrepid self-analysis, and the interpretation of dreams. The rest was genius!

––––––––––

The first and perhaps the most significant result of Freud's discovery was that it enabled him to overcome a mistake that he made in his early theory of the neuroses.

According to this early theory, an important role in the etiology of the neuroses was to be attributed to sexual seduction in the early years of childhood. Patients reproduced scenes from their early childhood in which some adult person sexually seduced them. With female patients, the part of the seducer was usually assigned to the father. It seemed that neurotic symptoms could be traced to these scenes of sexual seduction and assault on the part of a parent.[6]

Freud was, therefore, led to conclude that premature sexual experiences of this nature constituted sexual traumas. The experiences themselves seemed to have no effect at the time, but mental impressions of the experiences were retained, although they remained unconscious. The memory of the experience was reactivated at puberty, producing pathological results.

Since the memories underlying hysterical phenomena are absent from the patient's accessible recollections and are incapable of entering consciousness, neurotic symptoms were described as compromise formations resulting from a conflict between the memories of sexual traumas and a mental force tending to keep them repressed.

Three periods could therefore be described: a period in childhood when the sexual traumas occurred, a period of apparent health and successful defense against the reactivation of the memory of the traumas; and a failure of defense, accompanied by a return of the repressed.[7]

The error in this early theory arose from a failure to distinguish between patients' fantasies about their own childhood and real memories. The accounts of sexual seduction in childhood were then recognized to be fictitious.

This meant that Freud's original theory, to his profound dismay, went up in smoke. If the sexual seductions were fictitious, then there were no so-called traumas to account for the symptoms.

An analyst, interestingly enough, has attempted to revive the old seduction theory. He even went on to make the ridiculous claim that Freud attempted to conceal his knowledge of sexual abuse in childhood.

Freud never denied the existence of sexual seduction in childhood, but he learned that hysterical fantasies do not prove it always takes place in reality.

The discovery of this mistake and the discovery of the Oedipus complex saved the day. This was a pivotal, decisive turning point for psychoanalysis. It led to the realization that sexual impulses operated normally in children without the need for outside stimulation, i.e., seduction.

The Oedipus complex implies that children are capable of tender feelings toward one of their parents, and this would mean that such feelings were capable of being interpreted as seduction and assault at a later time. Since the seduction scenes related to premature sexual experiences in childhood, this would signify that the tender feelings were accompanied by erotic feelings as well.

When the seduction fantasies were subjected to analysis, the door was opened to an insight into the spontaneous manifestations of infantile sexuality. The whole range of the child's sexual life was subsequently uncovered.

The Infantile Period

When Freud turned to the current literature on sexuality, (which he studied carefully), in order to understand the perplexing sexual experiences of his patients; he found that sexuality was limited to and defined as adult genital sexuality. Children were conceived to be asexual beings, and sexual feelings were believed to occur, for the first time, at puberty.

Since this contradicted everything that Freud had learned from his studies of the neuroses, he synthesized existent sexual theory and his new findings to create a bold and extraordinary new theory of sexuality. This saw the light of day as the "libido theory," which Freud published in his THREE ESSAYS ON THE THEORY OF SEX, in 1905.[8]

The libido theory approximates the Greek conception of sexuality symbolized by the Greek God Eros. This is because it did not limit itself to the narrow confines of adult genital sexuality. The Pagan world idealized the sexual instinct as a positive, fertile life-giving power, whereas the Christian world idealized the sexual object; and denigrated the God Eros, clothing him in shame and guilt. The sexual instinct, in Freud's libido theory, is defined as an extensive pleasure seeking, procreative, love-inducing, vital erotic force.

In Freud's new theory, his most surprising innovation was the proposal that sexuality had an early maturation and efflorescence in infancy. This remarkable development is subject to the infantile amnesia covering our early childhood years (from birth to about age five) and is, therefore, unremembered. Sexuality, according to this theory, begins at birth and ends with death. Accordingly, the development of the sexual instinct was described as "biphasic," the first taking place in infancy and the second during the years of puberty.

The sexual drive in children was perceived to have different forms of expression than those found in the adult. However, their sexual nature was attested to by the fact that they produced the same erotic pleasure provided by adult sexual practices.

With exceptional concision he outlined the development of sexuality throughout the course of growth and development. He postulated early phases of oral, anal, and phallic stages of development; in which these "pregenital" erogenous zones played the principal role. In these infantile

13

stages of maturation, he was able to describe the different manifestations of sexuality, presentations that differed from adult, genital sexuality. Children were portrayed as polymorphous perverse.

The primal forms of sexuality persist, nevertheless, into maturity, and are only spuriously different from adult sexual conduct; precisely because they are incorporated into adult sexual life, like an old civilization buried underneath a new civilization. They surface clearly and are open to quotidian observation in adult sexual foreplay. Their presence had been observed of course, but other writers who studied sexuality had overlooked their significance.

Sexual energy is depicted as very plastic, labile, and mobile; an energy which can be displaced from one erotic aim to another or one person (object) to another, like an electric charge (cathexis). There are constant oscillations: progressions and regressions from early, primitive, atavistic modes of expression to mature refined aims and modes of expression. From coarse and crude lust to rarefied heights of tender, gentle intimacy. Processes of defense, sublimation, and aim-inhibition transform sexual energy.

Freud described Eros as a Janus faced God. One face bears the face of sensuality and the other the face of tenderness. Freud believed that tenderness itself could be explained as the result of the transformation (transmogrification?) of erotic tension by means of aim-inhibition and reaction formation. Sometimes, it is a reaction formation against sadism. It can also be conceived as the result of identification of with a tender parent.
One usually thinks of love as the epitome of altruism. And, so it is, when lovers sacrifice their own self-interest in favor of those that they love. But, the affairs of the human heart are more complicated then this would lead us to believe.

We are also capable of loving someone who reminds us of ourselves. Unconsciously, those that we love can be represented as the child that we once were or the person that we would like ideally to be or become. Consequently, our love for them is narcissistic. In fact, this is the one of the foundations of our love for our children. We love our children because they represent extensions of ourselves.

The contribution to love made by the Id, the realm of the instincts, looms large indeed; but it is matched by the contribution from our entire Self.

The Infantile Period

This takes the form of extending "ego libido" or narcissism from Self to others. The result is a transfer to others of the interest, concern, and care that we usually reserve for ourselves alone.

In his constant revision of the original theory, he added that the essence and ultimate meaning of Eros is the quest for union, oneness, and identification with the loved person. Passionate love pursues this quest. Along with the wish to return to the womb, whence we all came. The vagina is the inheritor of the womb.

This is an understanding of love that Freud knew corresponded closely to the remarkable idea of love of Plato, the great Greek philosopher, two millennia ago.

Love is <u>selective</u> by its very nature. To love everyone, is to love no one. Just as to be everywhere is to be nowhere. For this very good reason, Freud did not espouse the Sermon on the Mount of Jesus Christ that urged universal, indiscriminate love.

Mankind does not tolerate too much reality; particularly when it comes to sex (and money). Freud's new understanding of sexuality was greeted, of course, with shock, stupefaction, and nauseating hypocrisy by Victorian society, which did not believe that children could, would, or should have sexual feelings.

In terms of the antagonism, misunderstanding, and skeptical denials that it provoked, the libido theory ranks equally with the Oedipus complex, to be sure. It has failed to be understood and subsequently rejected by many dissident analysts. It was Karl Abraham that appreciated the libido theory best and contributed most to its further development and approfondissement.

The two theories do not stand alone. They require each other for mutual understanding and explanation. What is quite remarkable is that: after the libido theory was created because of the discovery of the Oedipus complex, it was used to explain the Oedipus complex itself.

The theory was used to explain the Oedipus complex in terms of the early stages of development of the sexual drive. This was hardly a simple task. In fact, Freud attempted to correlate stages of libidinal development and the Oedipus complex over a long period of time. This subject attracted his attention for his entire scientific career.

III. THE INFANTILE PERIOD

The Oedipus complex originates during the infantile period, but its effects persist throughout the lifetime of the individual. It is obvious that the content of Oedipal wishes differs depending on their presence in a child or in an adult. As mentioned previously, there is no <u>one</u> Oedipus complex; the complex of childhood continually changes producing different contents at different stages of life. The Oedipus complex, like the human mind, does not exist in space but only in time.

The estimate of the nature of the Oedipus complex in the child, however, is beset with special difficulties. To begin with, one is forced to talk of events that take place in childhood in terms that are only appropriate for adults in analysis. Therefore, it often seems comic and incredible when certain ideas and feelings are attributed to the child.

The love affair that a child has with a parent is different from a love affair between two adults. There are similarities to be sure, but there are very significant differences. This will be made clear later in this essay.

Secondly, our knowledge of events that occur in the child was drawn at first from the analysis of adults. As a result, a difficulty arises in distinguishing between events which take place in childhood and events that occurred at later periods and were projected into the past.

The attempt to overcome these difficulties produced two interpretations of the Oedipus complex. On the one hand, one could assume that patients projected their fantasies into the past, a process called retrogressive fantasy making, and that the events ascribed to childhood had never taken place at all. Or, on the other hand, one could assume that fantasies in the adult were based on real events that took place in childhood; and that these fantasies only served to distort the nature of these events.

Seymour Keitlen

Freud adopted the first alternative until certain developments led him to abandon the first view in favor of the second. We will now consider the evolution and motivation of this important change.

According to the libido theory in its early form, infantile sexuality consisted in the derivation of pleasure from the stimulation of erotogenic zones and from the satisfaction of certain components of the sexual instinct (e.g., voyeurism). The various sources of erotic gratification were said to pursue an independent course and were at first without an object; that is, the sexual drive was autoerotic. The finding of an object takes place for the first time at puberty, when the various elements are subordinated under the primacy of the genital zone.[9]

Since the first love choice occurred at puberty, the fantasies that occur at puberty could only cover the autoerotic activity occurring in childhood. The fantasies of puberty abound in seduction and assaults because the individual, as he grows up, attempts to efface the recollection of his autoerotic activities; and this he does by exalting their memory traces to the level of object love. Moreover, in constructing fantasies, the individual sexualizes his memories; that is, he brings commonplace experiences into relation with sexual activity and extends his sexual interest to them.[10]

The memories that the individual possesses of his childhood are "screen memories," which owe their value as a memory not to its own subject matter, but to the relation existing between that subject matter and some repressed psychic material.

Recollections of childhood are constructed from fantasies occurring at a later period. Our childhood memories, accordingly, show us our earliest years not as they were but as they appeared at later periods when the memories were formed.[11] This signifies that hatred against a father, for example, has been strengthened by a number of motives arising in later periods and other relationships in life; and that the sexual desires toward the mother have been molded into forms that would have been as yet foreign to the child.

According to this view, then, the Oedipus complex consisted, for the most part, in experiences of later periods projected back to the past.

There were two sources of information that decided the gradual modification of this view: the direct observation of children and the study of infantile neurosis. These two excellent sources of information were

18

The Infantile Period

decisively significant because they eliminated the distorting factor introduced by the process of retrogressive fantasy making.

When this factor was eliminated, it became clear that the Oedipus complex was a real episode indeed in the life of a child. It became clear that children form tender ties with both parents and experience jealousy, and rivalry.

This was something that Freud knew from the outset, but that he had to return to by a lengthy, roundabout route. It would be altogether absurd to believe that Freud did not know that children love their parents or that this had to be "discovered." This would have been the discovery of the obvious. No one finds it necessary to repress the childhood affection that one had for parents.

What he did not know and what he had to learn was that the child's love had erotic components, and that the passionate components produced the Oedipus complex.

With the benefit of retrospective hindsight, it seems that his own internal resistance to his own discoveries can account for his delayed progress through the maze of perplexing data. I do not say this with any depreciatory intent, however, because I am aware of sticky resistances of my own.

It is a tribute to Freud's genius that, even when he took a wrong path, he made important discoveries. This is exemplified by his ideas of retrogressive fantasy making and screen memories. These are both excellent and valid ideas. However, they no longer imply that the events of the childhood Oedipal drama are not real events; they no longer imply that they are only the product of fabrication at a later period.

The child claims from the objects of its affection all the signs of love that it knows of; and desires physical possession in all the ways that it has surmised in its fertile imagination.[12]

In addition, these two excellent sources revealed that the parents often exert an influence on the preference of the child by manifesting their own preferences.[13]

According to this standpoint, the Oedipus complex was a real situation in childhood and not merely a projection into the past of later experiences. The early libido theory was subsequently modified to include the fact that the early unfolding of infantile sexual life already gave rise to the choice of a love object.[14]

The basis of object choice in infancy was explained in terms of the first erotic gratifications that take place at that time. The child's experiences of gratification become the natural and biological source from which it chooses its love objects. We naturally love all sources of pleasure, and hate all sources of pain.

The first autoerotic sexual gratifications are experienced in connection with the vital functions in the service of self-preservation, and it is only later that the sexual instincts become independent of the ego instincts. It is, therefore, inevitable and perfectly normal that those persons who are concerned with the care and nurture of the child should become his earliest sexual love objects. In the first instance this is the child's mother or her substitute. This type of object choice was called "anaclitic"(to lean on).[15]

The direct observation of children and child analysis also resulted in a change in the definition of the complex; since they revealed that the child develops a tender as well as a hostile tie to the parent of the same sex. The existence of two contradictory feelings-love and hate -toward the same person was called ambivalence.[16]

Henceforward, the Oedipus complex came to mean the conjunction of a tender tie to one parent and an ambivalent tie to the other.

IV. THE PERIOD OF SEXUAL LATENCY

After a period of early efflorescence in childhood, the first configuration of a child's love that is coordinated with the Oedipus complex succumbs, from the beginning of latency onwards, to a wave of repression.

At first it seemed that the disappearance of the complex was due to a lack of fulfillment of Oedipal wishes, to its lack of success, and because of its inherent impossibility. In girls, it seems probable that these motives for the destruction of the complex are valid.

Since dreams revealed death wishes against parents, I am surprised that Freud, as far as I know, did not emphasize that these would produce retaliatory fears of death because of projection; which would also serve as a powerful motive for the passing of the complex, in both sexes.

What is more certain is that the disappointment of Oedipal wishes occasions feelings of loss of love, of Oedipal defeat, which are the basis for neurotic feelings of inferiority.[17]

In one of Freud's grand asides, he remarked that happiness is the fulfillment of childhood wishes. In this regard, it can be said that a great deal of the unhappiness of everyday life is due to a sense of Oedipal defeat- either in love or in work.

Further experience revealed that the dissolution of the complex in boys is due to the fear of punishment that it inherently contains. The Oedipus complex succumbs to the threat of castration.[18]

During the latency period, moral and aesthetic barriers are constructed which serve to check impulses which originated in the infantile period. The most important barrier is the barrier against incest.

Seymour Keitlen

Freud did not believe that the dread of incest could be explained in terms of individual psychology, He came to believe that the barrier against incest is probably among the historical acquisitions of mankind. In his book, <u>TOTEM and TABOO</u>, he presented a reconstruction of those events that might have led to the acquisition of incest dread.[19]

Because of the development of the incest interdiction, the original erotic attachment to the parents is given up and replaced by identifications with both parents. These identifications form the basis of many personality traits. The external authority of the parents is relocated into the self and forms the nucleus of conscience. The moral conscience, therefore, may be described as the heir to the passing of the Oedipus complex.[20]

The original erotic trends belonging to the complex are in part desexualized and sublimated, and in part also inhibited in their aims. They show themselves (for all the world to see) as purely, tender, affectionate, emotional ties that are no longer ostensibly erotic in character.

Although the constellation undergoes repression, it continues to exert an influence from the unconscious. Because of its continued unconscious existence, each individual finds a special individuality in the nature of the relations that he will have to people of his own and opposite sex. The nature of these relationships has been established during the first years of childhood.

The conditions, which governed parent-child relationships, the impulses and aims, justified in these relations form an infantile pattern, set or prototype which perpetually repeats itself as life goes on. This prototype or pattern is called an imago.

The repetition is brought about by the transfer of feelings and attitudes that were originally directed toward the parents to persons that resemble them and act as their surrogates.[21]

This means that attitudes and feelings originally concerning the Oedipus pattern are transferred to persons who act in place of the parents. That is to say, feelings of affection are relocated to persons resembling the parent of the opposite sex and ambivalent feelings, hostile and affectionate, are switched to persons of the same sex.

In the latency period, the persons who most readily become the object of these transferred feelings are the child's teachers, and the relationships between the child and his mentors serve as an excellent example of this process.

On the occasion of the celebration of the fiftieth anniversary of his Gymnasium, Freud delivered a charming address in his usual lucid style. It was entitled "Some Reflections on Schoolboy Psychology."

Here he pointed out that our relations with our teachers would be incomprehensible as well as inexcusable unless we related our behavior to its childish roots.

Teachers encounter sympathies and antipathies to the production of which they contribute very little. The real personality and conduct of the teacher plays a very small role in the production of the feelings and attitudes of their students.

Children exhibit an equal inclination to love and to hate them. They are capable of fiercely opposing them or excessively submitting to their authority.

Pupils show great curiosity about their personal lives and interests, their weaknesses, and their merits and demerits. Educators are taken as models of aspiration and behavior; or targets for hostile revolt. Idealization and identification are commonplace. Devaluation is rampant. We often feel guilty when we fail to meet the standards, goals, or demands of our schoolteachers.

The entire relationship is marked by ambivalence. And, this ambivalence can be explained by the fact that those who teach easily become parent substitutes who inherit relations that were established in infancy. The emotional attitudes toward them are derived from the infantile imagoes of the mother and father, i.e., from the unconscious images of the parents.[22]

We are capable of learning from our schoolteachers precisely because we love them. The need to be loved by our teachers provides the best motivation to learn. On the other hand, if we hate and resent them, we learn nothing at all, no matter how gifted the teacher.

Since teachers are taken as models for identification, they often play an exceptionally important role in our lives. This is well illustrated in Freud's life by his ambition to identify with Brucke, his distinguished professor of physiology, Heinrich Schliemann, the archeologist, and Charcot, the charismatic French neurologist. Freud played the same role in my own life. He is a father figure for every analyst, and one of his most appealing traits is his aggressive, masculine intellectual style.

V. THE TRANSFORMATION OF ADOLESCENCE

At puberty, the sexual instinct exerts its demands in full strength due to a reinforcement stemming from somatic sources. Since the only satisfactions that the child possesses pertain to those of childhood, a very intense flow of feeling toward the Oedipus network comes into force. The early incestuous objects of infancy are thus reanimated and invested with libido. Since the adolescent cannot immediately fulfill his reanimated desires with real persons, he does so with imaginary persons in fantasy.

In the fantasies of puberty, the infantile tendencies emerge once more, but they appear now in disguised forms due to the presence of the incest barrier.

The content of the Oedipus complex at puberty is proportional to the degree of somatic and ego development, since the sexual knowledge of the individual has been increased. Sexual experience on a genital level is also obtained, albeit with much fear and trembling.

In other words, Oedipal wishes during adolescence and afterwards are no longer the approximations of adult desires which existed in infancy. They represent unconscious genital desires to accomplish the deeds that Oedipus Rex did live out in the classic Greek tragedy. The play is no longer the caricature and exaggeration which it was in relation to the complex as it existed in childhood.

Adolescence is the disturbing transition period between childhood and adulthood. The essential task of puberty and adolescence, accordingly, is for the individual to free himself from his parents and his childhood, to disengage from the nuclear family.

This time-honored, scriptured necessity takes on new and profound meaning when it is realized that this signifies that the adolescent must master and overcome his Oedipus complex. What does this mean?

For a son, this consists in releasing his desires from his mother in order to employ them in quest of an external object in reality; and in reconciling himself with his father if he has remained antagonistic to him; or in freeing himself from his domination, if in relation to the infantile revolt, he has lapsed into excessive dependence. Independence, responsibility, and self-reliance then become the essence and hallmark of emotional maturity. The normal individual succeeds in this task.[23]

VI. APPLICATIONS

I have provided examples of the explanatory power of the Oedipus idea, briefly, and in passing. Several important summaries of applications follow; which show how Freud applied the idea to explain several important topics in psychoanalysis. This is the second period of Freud's work outlined in the introduction. Here we see Freud, en pleine forme, showing his complete mastery of theory and information.

NEUROSIS
The study of neurotic patients reveals that the detachment from the parents is not at all accomplished. A son remains, for example, in a state of subjection to his father all his life, and he is incapable of transferring his libido to a new sexual love object outside of the family. It is in precisely this sense that the Oedipus complex can be considered to be the nuclear complex of the neuroses.

The neurotic person who fails to overcome his Oedipal conflicts finds himself in a situation of sexual frustration. This can result from a persistence of the original parental attachment (fixation), or it may result from a return (regression) of the sexual drive to the initial attachment.[24] Fixation may be due to too little or too much maternal closeness. One wants what one is accustomed to having; or what one feels that one was unjustly deprived of. Whereas, regression is like a river that flows back into tributary channels when an obstruction lies in its forward path. Severe Oedipal conflicts are precisely and usually what lies in the path of maturity.

In hysteria, incestuous object choice is particularly prominent, and in obsessional neurosis, ambivalent feelings toward one of the parents are particularly in evidence. Obsessive-compulsive neurosis is the classic example of a neurosis produced by regression because of severe unresolved Oedipal conflicts. The regression is back to the anal sadistic stage of infantile sexuality. The symptoms represent a compromise formation of anal sadistic trends and characteristic defensive processes. The primary defenses are isolation, undoing, and reaction formation.

Since the neurotic individual fails to transfer his sexual desire to a new sexual object outside of the family, his libido is forced to seek gratification in fantasy life (a process called introversion). The finding of a person to love is a re-finding. New loves are old loves. Nouveau vin dans les vielles bouteilles. The transference of feelings from old family loves to new loves plays a large role in the unfolding of love.

The incestuous nature of the neurotic fantasies remains, of course, outside of conscious awareness because the incest barrier has been built during the latency period. The existence of this barrier requires every individual to find a way around it. Because of its presence, one is obliged to transfer feelings from a parent to someone outside the family; but it must be someone who does not remind one too much of the original object. Otherwise, anxiety would ensue. This is accomplished in innumerable ways.

This process of getting around the incest barrier was made clear to me by observing the marriage choices of several of my friends. An Iranian friend who was dark and swarthy found it necessary to marry a blond, blue-eyed girl from Holland, obviously very different in appearance from his mother. An Italian friend chose a fair complexioned woman, with auburn hair, who had just emigrated from Scotland. In spite of this maneuver, he became impotent after his marriage (he did not get all the way around the barrier). A Jewish colleague found his solution by marrying a girl of Chinese extraction. This also achieved the purpose of getting his parents very angry. It is not only the image of parents that has to be bypassed but also, at times, the images of brothers and sisters. And, it is not only physical characteristics that need to be avoided; but, what is more important, similar personality traits as well.

The sexual instinct is forced to invest those forms of sexual activity that were appropriate to the infantile period. The symptoms of neurosis, therefore, express in disguised form the libidinal trends of the infantile organization of Eros.

They represent compromise formations composed of sexual derivatives and defensive operations. The contribution to symptom formation of defensive processes or erotic discharge processes varies in degree in different symptoms. Either defense or discharge needs may be equally balanced, or one or the other may predominate. In phobias, defensive operations, obviously, predominate.

The neurotic being therefore has a peculiar and remarkable sex life. The sexual life of a neurotic person is, as odd as it may seem, actually made up by his symptoms; because the symptoms do offer some (if minimal) discharge of sexual energy.

This viewpoint implies that no specific or special causal factor need be found as the basis for neurosis. Because this view implies that the neurotic being falls ill in an attempt to solve the very same problems of the "normal" mortal. Everyone has Oedipal conflicts. The differences between the neurotic and the normal human being are therefore quantitative and not qualitative. It is all a question of degree, and not a question of kind.[25]

It has long been agreed that growing up in a loving family is the best prevention against neurosis. However, those that are so fortunate as to have grown up with loving parents still are subject to multiple accidental and unanticipated events in life that play a very influential role in the exacerbation of Oedipal conflicts. Accidental, adventitious events, therefore, can explain the development of symptoms during growth and development.

As a result of the intensification of conflicts, the self is left little alternative other than symptom formation. Under these circumstances, everyone does the best that he can; particularly because one or both elements of the causal intrapsychic conflicts are unconscious.

This decisive causal factor is illustrated by the parent in an unhappy marriage who compensates for this by overinvesting in one of the children. This can lead to increased incestuous or dependency conflicts in the child. Many exceptionally beautiful women pay a high price for their beauty, because it augments sensual feelings in male family members, which in turn can lead to early sexual seduction and its nefarious consequences. In two cases of authentic father-daughter incest that I studied, the consequence was not hysteria but psychosis. Hysteria seems to thrive on imaginary seduction in childhood.

A child who loses a parent in early childhood can react to this loss as the magical fulfillment of a hostile Oedipal wish, with its attendant increase of guilt feelings. Parents who are cruel and abusive to their children can increase parricidal and matricidal wishes. Another example is that sadistic parents who threaten their children with castration, of course, intensify this fear. Sexually inhibited parents with a too strict puritanical conscience efficiently increase sexual guilt in their offspring. Finally, one must not forget poor Daniel Paul Schreber, the paranoid judge who wrote an excellent account of his illness; who would not have fallen ill without the generous help of his sadistic father. Etc., etc..

We will return to the important topic of accidental factors in the etiology of neurosis later in this study.

The wonderful gift of human language may be what permits human thought to become conscious. This is because conscious thought is most closely associated with language. Human language, however, has its roots deep in the unconscious mind. It is therefore discernible that the repressed Oedipus complex is too central and important not to find expression in language. However, because of its tabooed content it is expressed, understandably, in profanity only.

Everyone is familiar, of course, with the word "motherfucker" (horrible dictum), although they would much rather that it not be mentioned. This term is used as a noun, verb, object, adjective, adverb, and participle. It is used to insult someone by accusing them of one's own unconscious desires. Use is obviously made of projection as a defense. This expression is a direct, uncensored, undisguised, striking derivative of incestuous wishes. It states clearly: "It is not I who want to do such a terrible thing, but it is you who want to do this dreadful thing." Its ubiquitous use testifies to the reality of the incestuous wishes of the Oedipus complex, even though proof of this reality is hardly needed at this point in time. It is amazing that this one word, deliberately ignored, can really be more convincing about the existence of the Oedipus complex than any recondite tome. Those who would doubt the existence of the Oedipus complex should ask themselves: "Why else, in this God forsaken world, would such an expression exist?"

The Origin of the Complex

Profane language, suppressed in "polite society," as the saying goes, also expresses many other unconscious desires derived from the various stages of infantile sexuality. It is a rich source of highly charged emotional expression and confirmation of infantile sexuality in all its subtle, hidden forms. In some individuals its incessant use amounts to a neurotic symptom, since it is used to discharge sexual tensions in speech.

THE PSYCHOLOGY OF LOVE
Freud defined the role of the complex in the selection of a person to love in his analysis of a special type of choice made by men. He described a special kind of selection characterized by a series of conditions of love and certain typical behavior toward the loved person. This type of object choice is frequently seen in the Don Juan personality. It is by no means rare or uncommon. It is a superb example of the exceptional explanatory power of the idea.

A specific and constant condition is the need for an injured third party. Men who make this type of choice in their love life choose a person in regard to whom another person has a right of possession. His love relations, therefore, always form a classic lover's triangle.

The second condition is that the loved partner be a woman who has a damaged reputation because of promiscuity and infidelity.

The first of these conditions allow the discharge of feelings of enmity against the third party of the triangle; the second allows for the expression of feelings of jealousy toward the woman.

The behavior of individuals of this type is also characteristic. The highest value is set on the woman whose reputation is not at all intact. She always represents the unique and irreplaceable beloved, or so it is claimed.

On the other hand, the individual who makes this type of choice invariably stresses his own fidelity, in spite of the fact that, in reality, intimate relationships of the same kind are started and ended, repeated and replaced in a long series. Lastly, he expresses a desire to rescue or save his lover from complete loss of respectability.

The characteristics that comprise this type of choice can be explained as a derivative of an infantile fixation of feelings of tenderness for the person's mother. They are a manifestation of the fact that the original attachment has persisted after puberty, and that the persons chosen are mother surrogates.

The first condition, the need for an injured third party, is explained by the fact that for a child the mother's belonging to the father is an inseparable part of her nature. In seeking a relationship where a third party is present, the individual recreates the situation in childhood.

The third party who becomes the object of enmity is, none other, than a representation of the father.

If it is true that the beloved chosen is really a mother substitute, then a long series also becomes quite comprehensible because a stand-in is never the mother herself. Throughout the series a search is made for the unconscious mother imago, which is simply unattainable in the realm of reality.

The explanation for the need to save is not as immediately comprehensible as the other features. The explanation of this feature can be derived, however, by the analysis of certain fantasies of saving, the analysis of these fantasies enables one to conclude that rescuing a woman acquires the significance of giving her a child or making one for her, and that the child in question is none other than the individual himself, since he identifies with his father [sic].[26]

SEXUAL IMPOTENCE

As we have already seen in the preceding discussion of neurosis, the sexual instinct may be turned from reality and absorbed into the life of fantasy. This process of introversion leads to the strengthening of the first sexual objects, and no advance is made in applying libido to extraneous persons in the real world. The whole current of erotic feeling may remain attached to unconscious incestuous objects or, to put it more accurately, may be fixated to incestuous fantasies.

If a sexual partner is reminiscent of an incestuous family object, sexual impotence is then employed as a defense against anxiety and guilt. The influence of the Oedipus complex is revealed in the format of the Hamlet scenario, mentioned earlier, in which there is an inability to perform a required action.

The Origin of the Complex

Persons suffering from impotence tend to emphasize their fear of sexual failure, whereas the true state of affairs is that they are really afraid of Oedipal success.

Sexual impotence and frigidity, of course, also occur when partners are consciously or unconsciously angry with each other, for reasons too numerous to mention. They then represent a passive aggressive defense against suppressed or repressed hostility.

A less severe condition occurs when some amount of sexual feeling actively remains. This becomes possible when the two currents of feeling involved in normal love, the sensual and tender currents, are dissociated. The use of this defensive maneuver, enables the individual to get around the incest barrier. The sensual feeling which is still active fixes on a person who does not inspire tender feelings, or the person chosen evokes tender feelings but remains erotically ineffectual. "When such men love they have no desire and when they desire they cannot love."[27]

This leads to an unhappy state of affairs; because, as Kierkegaard once remarked," there is passion without love, but no love without passion."

The person who is idealized and inspires Platonic love is an unconscious representative of the idealized infantile mother imago. Whereas, the partner who inspires lust is a representative of the unfaithful, degraded and devalued mother imago.

THE SEXUAL DEVIATIONS

Analysis of a certain fantasy, namely, a fantasy whose content is that "a child is being beaten," enabled Freud to raise the expectation that the sexual deviations or "perversions" are ramifications of the Oedipus complex. And, by analyzing a particular perversion, namely masochism, he sought to clarify the genesis of perversions in general. He sought to establish that all perversions could be derived from the Oedipus constellation.

To this end, masochism was seen as a constitutional reinforcement or premature growth of a single sexual component; but it was brought into relation with the child's Oedipus complex and understood as a "residue" or resultant of that complex.

If the analysis of this fantasy _"a child is being beaten"_ is traced through the early period to which it is referred and remembered; it shows that, then, the child was involved in his struggles with the Oedipal network of wishes.

When the complex was repressed, a sense of guilt appeared. The origin of this guilt is not known. There is no doubt, nonetheless, that this guilt is connected with incestuous wishes, and that it is justified by the persistence of these wishes in the unconscious.

It is noteworthy that Oedipal guilt is based on magical thinking, i.e., the belief that wishes are omnipotent equivalents of actions. Otherwise, their continued persistence in the unconscious would not cause guilt. Psychic reality prevails because of the persistence of magical thinking, which endows wishes with the power of actions.

When incest does actually take place in a family, the guilt that is produced is devastating and leads to serious pathology.

There is another factor operating here that has received insufficient attention and emphasis. Oedipal guilt and the need for punishment are not rational because it is based on wishes that are fulfilled in fantasy only. However, when the symbolic acting out of Oedipal wishes takes place with transference objects; it creates the illusion that the wishes have been fulfilled in reality, thereby creating and seemingly justifying guilt feelings.

In the history of the human family, on the other hand, incest and parricide were once social realities, and at that time guilt for Oedipal crimes was rational; leaving behind, perhaps, in the collective unconscious, memories and their attendant guilt feelings.

—————

The feeling of guilt is a necessary condition for the formation of masochism. Masochism can, accordingly, be viewed as a pursuit of punishment for incestuous wishes that were gratified by masturbation, with its attendant Oedipal fantasies in childhood.

The Origin of the Complex

In sexual masochism the punishment is provided by a sexual partner, whereas, in moral masochism the individual's conscience provides the requisite punishment.

Since Oedipal guilt is quite ubiquitous, it cannot, of course, be the only determinant for the phenomenon of masochism. The second requirement for the development of masochism is the remarkable wish to be treated like a woman. Masochism expresses homosexual wishes. However, masochism expresses feminine wishes that take a peculiar and special form. The masochist wants to be treated as if he were a woman who is being hurt: castrated, humiliated, degraded and abused in sexual intercourse.

The singular and unusual form of these wishes can be explained by the persistence of the primal fantasy of the" sadistic misconception of coitus." The origin and significance of this fantasy will be discussed below and in the next section.

Freud devoted a great deal of study to the phenomena of masochism and sadism. He wrote three papers on the topic of masochism alone. His views were continually and drastically modified. He began by describing masochism as being the result of sadism being turned on the self. In his final picture, he formulated the idea of a "primary" masochism that was a reflection of a hypothetical death instinct. Sadism was then seen as the death instinct turned outward. Other analysts, including myself, have never accepted the idea of the death instinct. Therefore, the following viewpoint is my own and is not attributable to Freud.

The sadistic misconception of sex provides, I believe, the Rosetta stone for the understanding of certain aspects of masochism, sadism, paranoia, and repression that would otherwise remain obscure. I am not sure, but I tend to believe that Freud did not appreciate just how important his discovery of this fantasy was.

Freud attributed the formation of this fantasy to the fact that children are naturally excluded from observing parental sexual life. They are therefore obliged to construct theories, in their imagination, about what takes place behind closed doors. When children, subsequently, overhear sexual intercourse, they mistakenly interpret what they hear to mean that their parents are hurting each other.

It is true that it can sound that way, but I do not believe that it always sounds that way. This could not explain the universality of this influential "primal fantasy."

The above explanation has to be complemented with the idea that a child's narcissism is offended by the idea that its parents are giving each other pleasure from which it is excluded. It therefore prefers to believe that they are hurting each other. This imaginative product serves as a balm to the child's injured narcissism.

This factor, while important, does not go far or deep enough. The fantasy is constructed by the child's endowing his parents with his own hostile wishes. Since the child harbors ambivalent emotions toward both parents, the sadistic fantasy allows for the wish fulfillment of each class of feeling. The child can then vicariously enjoy the fulfillment of his own hostile wishes by identifying with one or both parents in the fiction created by his own imagination.

This fabrication, which expresses an inseparable fusion of love and hate, acts as a blueprint for sexual identification with parents. That is to say, children want to identify with the imagined erotic activity of one or both of their parents in the sadistic fantasy.

This is illustrated by sadism as a sexual deviation that represents a blend of ambivalent feelings of love and hate. Sadistic behavior is used defensively by means of "identification and, secondly, sadism can be traced to the identification with one or both parents in the template of the sadistic misconception of coitus, to fulfill its characteristic sensual wishes.

One version of the sadistic fantasy of sex consists in portraying the parental sexual act as a violent crime or a murder. Therefore, the widespread interest in detective stories and who-done-it crime stories is unconsciously decided by sexual curiosity and the sadistic misconception of coitus.

———————

The sadistic conception of sex is by no means limited to children or "perversions." Rape can be understood as the acting out in adulthood of childhood sadistic fantasies. The exceptional prevalence and influence of this primal fantasy is betrayed by profane sexual language, which, again, is deliberately ignored by polite society.

The commonplace fact is that the word "fuck" is used as the leading colloquial expression for sexual intercourse internationally. It is a direct uncensored derivative of the sadistic misconception of coitus. It has many synonyms, all equally sadistic, like the words "bang," "ball," or "screw." The corresponding term for a penis is "prick," i.e., an instrument that harms.

The verb "to fuck" expresses the sadistic union of ambivalent feelings of love and hate. It essentially verbalizes wishes to harm or hurt; along with a simultaneous sexual instinctive desire, divorced from any tender sublimation.

This all too common word provides a rather sad commentary on the fact that its ubiquitous use testifies to the difficulty so many people have to attain a post ambivalent stage of sexual object relations. (cf. Octavio Paz, The Labyrinth of Solitude).

The preceding viewpoint also helped to throw light on the sense of guilt in neurosis; for this sense of guilt could now be related to forbidden incestuous wishes which persisted in the unconscious mind. Neurotic persons make masturbation at puberty the central point of their guilt feelings. The analysis of masochism made it evident that this sense of guilt relates to the onanism of early childhood, and not to that of puberty. It is to be connected not with the acts of masturbation themselves, but with the Oedipal wishes discharged in contemporaneous fantasies.[28] Several excellent female analysts have pointed out that the emotion of shame that can accompany masturbation is derived from the homosexual content of the masturbation fantasies.

HOMOSEXUALITY
One may very well wonder whether or not the feelings embodied in the Oedipus complex are reversible by experiences occurring after childhood? The answer seems to be that the feelings are capable of being reversed, and that this is what occurs in the genesis of homosexuality.

Seymour Keitlen

In the case of male homosexuality, an intense fixation upon the mother in the sense of the Oedipus complex occurs before puberty. This love for their mother plays a large role in the genesis of homosexuality. After puberty and adolescence, however, this fixation is abandoned in favor of identification with the mother.

Contrary to popular belief, homosexual men have a great love for women, although they cannot make love to women. Their fear of women and their fear of a woman's genitals overthrow their love for them. Consequently, their original childhood fixation is abandoned at puberty.

Homosexuality essentially involves a resolution of Oedipal conflicts and a defense against castration anxiety by means of the renunciation of the mother as a love object. The homosexual's love for his mother is then replaced by identification with the relinquished mother. Feminine identification is the condition sine qua non of male homosexuality. The reversal consists in substituting identification for object love, and in a reversal in the gender of the object that is chosen to be loved.

However, this is not strictly accurate because object love and identification with this object are not mutually exclusive. It is not a question of either/or. They coexist in different degrees; and when identification replaces object love, it is the erotic object that is exchanged while the original affection is retained. This is exemplified by the intense affection for his mother shown by Marcel Proust.

This is shown by the fact that homosexuals continue to love their mothers, (a little too much perhaps). Objects and wishes can be relinquished; but they do not perish--- they live on in the subterranean unconscious.

The active homosexual then makes a "narcissistic" object choice. He does this by choosing a male person to love who resembles himself and on whom he can bestow such love and care that he experienced from his own mother.[29] It is therefore understandable that little boys are chosen to fulfill this particular need.

The above formulation does not apply to all homosexuals. Other kinds of homosexuals choose persons who remind them of women, so that they can fulfill with them heterosexual desires that never perish. This is only made possible because the presence of a penis in their feminine appearing partners counteracts their fear of the "castrated" and castrating woman.

The Origin of the Complex

Active and passive roles are interchanged, and both partners identify with each other so that both active-masculine and passive-feminine modes can be vicariously enjoyed.

In a case of female homosexuality analyzed by Freud, a similar reversal of the Oedipus complex was found to lie at the basis of a homosexual change. The young woman in question turned away from her father and from men altogether after experiencing a great disappointment regarding her original unconscious love for her father.[31]

The vicissitudes of homosexuality help to explain many other psychological phenomena. Men are dreadfully afraid to acknowledge the homosexual component of their selves because they perceive it as an alarming threat to their masculinity. This is caused by the belief that feminine wishes imply identification with a castrated, inferior, devalued mother imago. Homosexual feelings, above all else, are therefore deeply repressed and vigorously denied by men, and they become a rich, fertile source of pathology.

Alcoholism and drug addiction are masochistic phenomena. The self-punitive and self-destructive component is obvious. Whereas, the homosexual component is seldom addressed; therefore, these conditions are seldom helped by therapy.

As was emphasized above, when homosexual wishes sexualize self-punitive behavior, it leads to masochism. When homosexuality is repressed and denied, feelings of love and/or hate can be projected; this leads to paranoia.[32]

The sexual abuse fantasy in hysteria contains a concealed fulfillment of an incestuous heterosexual wish, and guilt is avoided by portraying the seduced person as the innocent <u>victim</u> of seduction and abuse.

In a similar fashion, the paranoid persecutory fantasy represents a wish fulfillment of a homosexual <u>masochistic</u> wish. When masochistic wishes are projected, they are perceived as sadistic wishes in others. The paranoid person, like the hysteric, portrays himself also as an innocent victim, and makes use of the sadistic idea of sex. It is noteworthy how the sadistic notion of sex also helps to keep the underlying homosexuality concealed.

If an ambivalently loved person of the same sex is <u>lost</u>, an identification with the lost person often takes place. In a certain sense, the lost person then lives on, and grief is diminished.

When hostile feelings toward the "introject" are accordingly turned on the self, depression is produced (cf. "Mourning and Melancholia"). The guilt-ridden self is then treated sadistically by the person's conscience. As painful as depression most certainly is, it satisfies multiple ambivalent wishes. The psychological gain resides in the fulfillment of repressed hostile wishes toward the lost loved one, and the pain satisfies the need for punishment. This, however, is not the whole story.

It is quite remarkable that profane language, once again, accurately expresses the contribution of the sadistic concept of sex in depression. It does so in the following two ribald alliterations: the depressed individual feels that "he has been fucked by the fickle finger of fate" or "damned by the dangling dick of destiny." Both fate and destiny are well-known father symbols. Therefore, these phrases faithfully voice the <u>masochistic</u> psychological gain of depression, namely, the fulfillment of the need to be loved by the father. And, they express it better than psychoanalytic jargon.

<u>TRANSFERENCE</u>
It has been previously remarked that the relations that are established in infancy create feelings and attitudes that are later transferred to other figures. Since the most significant of a child's relationships are those comprised in the Oedipal triangle; it is comprehensible that the Oedipus complex contributes a very large share of the feelings that are later displaced. Our first example of this fascinating phenomenon was provided by the displacement made by students to their teachers.

Transference takes place, of course, in all human relationships.

One of the most enlightening, however, is the displacement that patient's make between their parents and their therapists.

The transference is said to be positive as far as it involves the transfer of friendliness, trust, confidence, affection, and respect onto the analyst. It is negative when it involves the relocation of hostile, aggressive feelings and attitudes.

The Origin of the Complex

The phenomenon not only helps to explain the nature of the psychotherapeutic effect of treatment, but it has proven to be one of the most important sources of insight in to the nature of the relations that were originally present between parent and child.

This process represents another illustration of the effects of the Oedipus complex, because in analysis, instead of remembering certain feelings and states of mind of his previous life, the patient reproduces them, lives through them again during the course of treatment. When this occurs it provides excellent information for the deductive reconstruction of the original events that took place in childhood.

If the patient is a man, he usually takes his material from his relationship with his father, in whose place he now puts the treating person. In so doing, he builds his resistance out of his struggles to attain personal independence, out of his ambition, and out of his disinclination to gratitude, the earliest aim of which was to equal and to excel his father.

These early feelings of hostile rivalry express themselves in the person's desire to criticize the analyst and psychoanalysis in general, his lack of cooperation, and in his wish to make the therapist feel impotent and to triumph over him.

This type of transference paradigm, incidentally, can also be fruitfully applied to the dissident analysts (e.g., Otto Rank) who left the "orthodox" movement to create their own versions of psychoanalysis.

Women who use a seductive erotic transference from their fathers to obstruct the cure also illustrate this process.[33]
An erotic transference is a negative transference.

The psychotherapeutic effect of psychoanalysis is a product of transference. This is not the same as a "transference cure," because the transference is analyzed. Just as a child learns from the teacher that he loves; so a patient only learns from an analyst toward whom his transference is positive. In this sense, psychoanalysis is a cure by love. Analytic treatment is a process of emotional reeducation; and every analyst is ideally an educator. It is an education that can lead to self-realization.

Moreover, the analysis of transference became the basic strategy of treatment, because its analysis in the here and now offers the best means of achieving conviction about unconscious past events.

It follows from the foregoing that, since psychotic patients cannot form an adequate positive transference; they cannot be helped by analytic treatment, in spite of heroic attempts to the contrary.

VII. THE ORIGIN OF THE COMPLEX

Freud developed two theories concerning the origin of the complex: a phylogenetic theory and an ontogenetic theory.

According to the first theory, the Oedipus complex was ultimately the product of events that took place in the early history of the human race. According to the second theory, the complex is ultimately the result of a set of biological circumstances and their psychological consequences. First, that the human child grows and develops in a family with its intimate triangular relationships. Second, that the human child is dependent on its parents for a long period of time. Lastly, the existence of a sexual unfolding in infancy during the period of dependency.

The two different theories are not mutually exclusive, since constitutional and accidental factors complement each other.
Moreover ontogeny recapitulates phylogeny, at least in embryology. Freud therefore never abandoned the phylogenetic view, but his later writings are characterized by a renewed effort to explain the facts on a pure ontogenetic basis.

A. THE PHYLOGENETIC THEORY
The Oedipus complex, as we have described it so far, implies that the child exercises a sexual preference in regard to its parents.

A theory of the origin of the complex would have to explain this gender preference. It would be difficult to explain in terms of the experiences of the child because it occurs at a time when its sexual knowledge is too limited to make this possible. Freud's studies had already made it clear that the child's intense sexual curiosity does not lead to a knowledge of the sexual facts of life.

Certain material found in the analysis of infantile neurosis provides a clue to the origin of this sexual preference. In these analyses, Freud found it difficult to dismiss the view that some sort of hardly definable sexual knowledge, something approximating an understanding, is at work in the child.

An example would be the observation that boys wish to break into their mother or enter her body in some way. Furthermore, with boys a wish to beget a child from their mother is never absent, with girls the wish to have a child from their father is equally constant, all this in spite of their being completely incapable of forming any clear idea of the means of fulfilling these wishes.

He found it difficult to form a conception of this sexual knowledge, but he believed it could be grasped by the excellent analogy to the extensive instinctive sexual knowledge of animals. This suggested that human beings also possess an instinctive endowment that is concerned with the processes of sexual life.[34]

There are other facts that point in this direction.

Individual symptoms, individual dreams, and individual fantasies can be explained by connecting them to the person's experiences.

However, there are typical symptoms, dreams, and fantasies that are difficult to connect with the individual's life or to relate to special events in the past.

If the individual forms of these mental products are so unmistakably connected with the person's experiences, it appears plausible that the typical forms are related to experiences that are themselves typical, universal, and common.

As a matter of fact, this does not prove to be the case because one cannot connect typical symptoms, dreams, or fantasies
to identical experiences that are common to different individuals. As a result, no explanation is immediately available concerning their origin, their necessity, and their recurrence.[35]

The Oedipus complex itself cannot always be traced back to experiences in the past life of the individual, nor can it always be related to a special situation in the past.[36]

The Origin of the Complex

Typical forms of neurotic symptoms, dreams, fantasies, and the Oedipus complex must, nonetheless, be based on material drawn from somewhere. Since they could not be traced back to the experience of the individual, it became at least plausible to believe that they were drawn from material that represented actual occurrences in the history of the human family.

What was originally produced by certain circumstances in prehistoric times would then have been transmitted in the shape of a schema that enables the person to fill in the gaps in his personal experience by using the experience of the past. This archaic inheritance or "phylogenetic memory" would thus represent a part of every mortal's endowment. This conforms to Lamarckian theory, and it is similar to Jung's idea of the "collective unconscious."

From this point of view, whenever one seemed to see traces of the aftereffects of an infantile impression, one should rather have to assume that one was faced by the manifestation of some constitutional factor or predisposition that had been phylogenetically created.[37]

In TOTEM AND TABOO, some experiences were described that might form part of a phylogenetic memory. Freud attempted to trace the current dread of incest and Oedipal guilt to a historical deed that took place in the history of the human family. That real historical happening was: the murder of the clan father, parricide.

Cultural anthropologists believe that the social conditions that prevailed in prehistoric times are unknown, because there is simply insufficient data for their reconstruction. They took place a very long time ago, around fifty millennia ago.

Freud relaxed his usual inner restrictions against philosophic speculation and produced an intriguing phylogenetic hypothesis. He speculated that men lived in groups in what he called a primal horde. A dominant male or leader fathered the offspring within the polygamous group. However, sexual access to the women in the group by offspring was not allowed; and was punished by castration. Consequently, and inevitably, this led to sexual rivalry among the consanguineous members of the group. The sexual frustration of the sons led to their banding together in order to murder the father or group leader.

This momentous violence was followed, however, by regret, remorse, and guilt, since the father of the clan was loved, admired, and respected as a protector and leader of the clan.

———————

Freud based his speculations on his analysis and interpretation of Totemism, a system prevalent in some primitive cultures.

In the Totem system, a group or clan worshipped a Totem animal, admired for its fear-inspiring strength. The identity of clan members was derived from their membership in a group designated by a particular Totem animal. Members of the clan were forbidden to marry other members of their own clan. This implied that the Totem system was evolved in order to avoid incest, because the prohibition against clan intermarriage effectively resulted in the avoidance of marriage of consanguineous members of the same clan.

Incest became Taboo by virtue of this prohibition, accompanied by a dread of incest, a dread so commonly found in neurosis.

The Totem system involved the celebration of a regular ritual called the Totem meal. In this ritual the Totem animal was killed and ceremoniously eaten by all the members of the clan.

Freud interpreted this to mean that the celebration of the Totem meal was a commemoration and symbolic repetition of the original murder of the clan father. The oral incorporation served several different ends. It represented an identification with the Totem animal and his protective strength. It provided for a sharing of the guilt produced by the original parricide. And, the participation of all clan members in the ritual formed a repeated affirmation of the commitment to the incest prohibition.

———————

This suggested that incest, parricide, and castration were real events in the early history of the human family.
The ritual Totem meal served to keep alive the memory of past historical events in succeeding generations. These rituals gradually died out, but a

phylogenetic memory of the original events remained as an archaic inheritance. However, this view assumes that experiences took place at one time in the far distant past and had an effect on later generations that knew nothing about these happenings. The modus operandi, which enabled a psychic continuity of this nature to operate throughout a series of generations remains both obscure and unknown.[38]

Freud consequently considered it a methodological error to use phylogenetic explanations before the ontogenetic possibilities were completely searched for and exhausted.

His later work on this topic, which we will take up, represents a new attempt to explain the Oedipus complex from the point of view of individual psychodynamics. Nonetheless, the phylogenetic view was not totally discounted, since he had always attempted to explain the neuroses in terms of the interaction of constitutional factors and the accidental, fortuitous events of personal experience. The phylogenetic view is the only idea that throws some light on the constitutional factor.

B. THE ONTOGENETIC THEORY

All of Freud's work from 1923 on testifies to a renewed effort to explain the origin of the Oedipus complex in terms of events that take place in the early years of childhood. This renewed effort was decided by an attempt to correlate the complex with the idea of human bisexuality. The result of this effort was the introduction of an important change in his conception of the complex, which was introduced in THE EGO AND THE ID, in 1923.

Additional impetus was derived from the work of female analysts who contributed important knowledge concerning the Oedipus complex in girls. As a matter of fact, almost all of Freud's early writings were marked by descriptions that pertained to the complex in males. Perhaps this is related to the fact that one of his major sources of information was always his own self-analysis. Be that as it may, the important contributions of female analysts led to a series of studies of female sexual development and a more detailed and thorough description of those events that lead to the constellation in girls.

1. THE COMPLETE COMPLEX

Up until the present time, we have described the Oedipus complex in the child as consisting of an affectionate love relationship to the parent of the opposite sex and an ambivalent, i.e., hostile and affectionate tie to the parent of the same sex. This description is adequate for most purposes, but it represents a simplification and schematization of a reality that is rendered far more complicated by the presence of a bisexual constitution in each individual.

Closer study reveals that the Oedipus complex does not always develop in this way, but that very often the relationships are inverted. Moreover, the tendencies of both forms can be found in the same person.

To help distinguish the possibilities and describe them intelligibly, the situation described above is termed the positive complex and the inverted form is called the negative complex. Homosexuality in both sexes expresses the negative or inverted form.

The complete complex, accordingly, is twofold: positive and negative. This is a product of human bisexuality.

This amounts to saying that a boy develops not only an ambivalent attitude toward his father and an affectionate love bond with his mother, but, at the same time, he also behaves like a girl and displays an affectionate feminine attitude toward his father and a corresponding hostile jealousy of his mother. Analytic experience then shows that one of these two constituents of the complex disappears, so that a series can be formed with the normal positive Oedipus complex at one end and the inverted negative one at the other. The intermediate members of the series will exhibit the complete type with one or the other of its constituents predominating. The relative preponderance of the child's relationship to one of the parents will reflect the intensity within him of one or the other of the two sexual predispositions.[39]

It is not all that complicated, since, in other simpler words, one can say that the individual has both male and female propensities, and one of the two dispositions manifestly predominates and the other is usually latent, potential, and concealed. We identify with both parents; and have ambivalent feelings toward both parents.

2. FINAL SYNTHESIS

The following is Freud's last formulation of the historical antecedents of the complex, after a half century of research.

According to the previous definition of the Oedipus complex, children form affectionate and erotic bonds with both parents. This removes the necessity for assuming that the child exercises a gender preference; and it leaves open the way to an explanation of the origin of the complex in terms of conditions and events that take place in childhood.

The processes that are involved are not altogether clear, but it seems that the little boy develops a love for his mother at a very early age. This results from the fact that it is his mother who is responsible for his nurture, care, and protection. Satisfaction of biological, self-preservative needs also provides the first erotic gratifications.

Nature has seen to it that the needs for survival are met by adding erotic pleasure to their fulfillment. The satisfaction of all biological requirements is accompanied by pleasure. This is why Eros is accurately defined as a vital force.

The child's mother, accordingly, becomes charged with pregenital libido. A mother represents a loved person based on this anaclitic model. At the same time, a boy loves his father very much. He is seen as a protector, and the child admires him, takes him as a model, and imitates his behavior.

Imitation is followed by identification. He therefore identifies with his father. For a time, these relationships exist side by side.

The child, then, has two psychologically distinct parental ties: an affectionate and erotic bond with his mother and an identification with his father.

As the boy's passionate feelings for his mother become more intense and as he learns more about the relationship between his parents; identification with the father takes on a hostile coloring since he is regarded as a rival and obstacle to the exclusive possession of the mother. A wish is thereby engendered to get rid of the father and to take his place with the boy's mother. This wish is reinforced by the identification with the child's father, since the complete identification would mean [sic] replacing the father in his relations with his mother.

49

The Oedipus complex, consequently, has its ultimate origin in the confluence of the paternal identification and the maternal love bond.[40]

Certain components of the sexual drive are directed toward an object from the beginning and retain this object in the course of growth and development (e.g., sexual curiosity, voyeurism). Other elements that are connected with erotogenic zones only have an object in the beginning, so long as they are dependent on the nonsexual functions. The objects are later given up when they are detached from these functions. They are not relinquished totally and can be regressively revived, e.g., men and women never give up their desire to suckle at the breast, which they return to in sexual foreplay.

Thus the first object of the oral impulse is the mother's breast, which satisfies nutritional and erotic, needs. The oral, incorporative impulse then becomes autoerotic.[41] This is exemplified by the transition from nursing at the breast to autoerotic thumb sucking.

The endowment of the mother with erotic feeling and the subsequent Oedipus constellation is only possible, accordingly, when all the sexual currents become directed toward a single person and when their diverse aims are organized and integrated.

This phase of development produces an infantile genital organization of sexuality---the "phallic phase." An organization that is manifested by infantile masturbation that has two components: a physical act and a complementary mental group of fantasies.

A child's sexual life at this time, however, is by no means exhausted by masturbation, for the masturbation is merely the discharge in the genital zone of an excitation belonging to the Oedipus complex. Oedipal wishes are discharged in masturbation fantasies. It is precisely this connection between masturbation and Oedipal fantasies that gives masturbation its significance.

The sexual needs are not only assured by direct stimulation of the genital zone. All the indirect forms of expression of affection that is bestowed on the child unfailingly have an effect on the genital zone as well.

The Origin of the Complex

The Oedipus complex is, accordingly, contemporaneous with the phallic phase. The sexual activity of this phase is the closest approximation possible in childhood to the final form of sexual life at puberty.[42]

Maternal loving care unwittingly acts seductively to elicit incestuous desires in the child. Children are quite gifted as well in the arts of seduction.

Now that the scales have fallen from our eyes, the erotic relationship of mother and child is open to everyday observation. The nursing, hugging, fondling, pinching, kissing, cooing, cuddling, caressing possessiveness show the passionate nature of the relationship quite clearly.

However, maternal care with its attendant affectionate and erotic gratifications must be understood to be a means of teaching the child how to love. The child can experience this pristine love relationship as a seduction. It provides the true basis, source, and kernel of truth for later hysterical fantasies of seduction.

Along with the dissolution of the complex due to the threat of castration by the father, the intense incestuous love of the mother must be given up.

Its place may be filled by one of two things: either an identification with the mother or an intensified identification with the father. The latter is the more normal because it allows the affectionate relation to the mother to be maintained without the erotic component. Nonetheless, the alternate outcome is possible.

A little boy, after he has had to relinquish his mother as an erotic object, will bring his femininity into prominence and identify himself with his mother. That is, with the person who has been lost, instead of with his father. In this way, the Oedipal network becomes inverted to the negative form, creating homosexuality. This is one of the ways that bisexuality takes a hand in the subsequent history of the Oedipus complex.[43]

There is no direct simple parallel between what occurs in the two sexes. The mother is, of course, the first person to be loved by the little girl, since she is also cared for and nurtured by the mother and invested with pregenital libido. Female analysts amply stressed this.[44]

Since the girl's original object of love is not retained, the origin of the Oedipal situation in girls raises one more problem in girls than it does in boys. It becomes necessary to explain how the young girl gives up her mother and takes her father as a beloved, thereby creating the Oedipal set.

The solution of this problem is contained in the idea of the castration complex in women that precedes and prepares for the development of the Oedipus complex. The girl's transition from the mother to the father is a result of the anatomical distinction between the sexes and the unconscious psychological consequences of perceived sexual differences.

A castration complex in girls relates to the finding that little girls notice the anatomical distinction between the sexes, i.e., they notice the penis of a brother, a playmate, or an animal. They then mistakenly imagine that they also possessed a penis at one time, but that their punitive mothers had taken it away. Whereas boys fear castration as a future punishment for Oedipal wishes, young girls experience a sense of castration as a fait accompli.

From the time of the creation of this unconscious belief, girls fall victim to penis envy.

Women find this idea as difficult to accept as men find the acceptance of their homosexuality. It is vigorously denied, and has led to the accusation that Freud was a male chauvinist. It is reacted to as a narcissistic affront because it is erroneously seen as a "put-down" of women and an implication that men are superior to women. It is perceived as male chauvinist propaganda rather than a scientific theory.

The fact that a man has female wishes does not imply that he is not really a man. Similarly, the fact that women have active-male wishes and wishes to be a man does not imply that women are inferior to men. Since women do feel unconsciously inferior to men, they are led to defensively reject the idea of penis envy.

Women readers will certainly be glad to hear, I am sure, that little boys (and grown men) also suffer from penis envy. They envy the larger penis of their fathers or other men, but comfort themselves with the knowledge that their penis will grow larger when they grow up. Some little girls comfort themselves with the belief that their clitoris is a "little penis," since they have no way of knowing that it is not a vestigial organ. There are pathological states in preadolescent girls who insist that they will grow up to be a male.

Little girls perceive the idealized penis of the phallic phase to be an incomparably better instrument for masturbation than a clitoris. In the primitive mind bigger is always better. The grass is always greener on the other side of the street. N'est ce pas?

All this in spite of the fact that women are can have multiple orgasms and men cannot. All this in spite of being endowed with a beautiful body, a longer life span than men, and, last but not least---a marvelous capacity to conceive and bear children (which capacity men envy, of course).

The little girl nevertheless gives up her wish for a penis and replaces it with a wish for a child, and with this purpose in view, she takes her father for a love object and her mother then becomes the object of her jealousy.[45]

There is a fundamental difference between the relation between the Oedipus complex and the castration complex in the two sexes. Whereas in boys, the complex succumbs to the threat of castration; in girls it is made possible by the castration complex. In girls, the motive of castration fear in the destruction of the complex is lacking. The effect of her castration complex is to force the female child into the Oedipal drama.[46]

Because castration fear is not present in women as a motive for the passing of the complex, Freud believed that, after the dissolution of the Oedipus complex and the internalization of parental authority, women had a weaker conscience than men. Here, I would agree with female critics that Freud was mistaken. Powerful motives for the passing of the complex in young women do exist, and they have been described earlier in this study. The moral and ethical conscience of women is not weaker than that of men, on the contrary, it is men who have been responsible for the greatest crimes in history.

Moreover, women do experience a subtle form of castration anxiety; in a form that is easily and usually overlooked. Castration anxiety in women takes the form of being afraid that their "castrated" state will be at some time revealed and exposed. Therefore there is a need to hide the female genital and there is an appreciation of pubic hair.

The preceding account represents a synopsis of Freud's final formulations of the historical antecedents and development of the Oedipus complex in terms of individual psychology and psychodynamics.

This narrative certainly provides an excellent and masterful explanation of the origin and development of the Oedipus complex. It is the product of Freud's lengthy years of painstaking and patient research.

Freud presented it in a tentative, circumspect fashion since he did not seek to formulate a dogmatic, closed philosophic system but a scientific theory that required continuing research.

He starts out by saying that because children love both of their parents, this removed the necessity of assuming that a sexual preference existed in the child. However I believe that a gender preference does exist in children.

This is related to the fact that the child's love for its parents is by no means equal in quality or quantity. The mother is the preferred sexual object for both girls and boys. Precisely because it is the mother's primary role to be devoted to the nurture and care of the child. One cannot compare the time and attention paid by fathers to their children to that spent by their mothers. And, as we have seen, it is the anaclitic gratifications experienced during this maternal care and devotion that creates the first sexual gratifications and feelings of love.

Moreover, children know that they came out of their mother's body, that they were once part of her, that she gave them life, although they do not accurately know how they got in there in the first place. Children respond with love to the fact that their mothers treat them as an extension of themselves. It is this narcissistic transfer that forms the basis for the development of the tender aspect of the emotion that we call love.

This unique experience illustrates the difference previously mentioned: between a love bond of a child and a parent and a love relationship between two adult lovers. Adult lovers do not provide each other with life or parental care. And, children do not have explicit sexual relations with their parents. The nature of the relationship is, accordingly, dissimilar, in spite of transference. One must therefore be cautious about applying ideas about adult relationships to relations between children and parents.

The Origin of the Complex

In the case of the little boy, therefore, his gender preference for his mother over his father is more than adequately explained by the decisive and overwhelming importance of maternal love and care.

Furthermore, the sexual instinct is essentially a reproductive drive. It is highly plausible that there exists an instinctive hereditary sexual endowment that leads to a gender preference for the opposite sex, because this would clearly serve procreative ends and the survival of the species. The erotic instinct is a biological drive, and sexual anatomy provides for a reproductive hand and glove relationship between the sexes. The hereditary endowment of instinctive knowledge about sexual processes is less in humans than it is in animals. Why this is so remains a mystery.

In the case of the female child, her equally intense love for her mother makes it all the more necessary, a plus forte de raison, to understand how this initial gender preference is given up and transferred to her father.

The preceding explanation provided by Freud for this shift, namely, the wish for a child that replaces a wish for a penis, is accurate; and it probably represents the deepest motive for the transition from the mother to the father. However, it deserves to be amplified by other factors, and it is certainly over determined.

The transition made by the little girl from her love for her mother to her love for her father is the result of push and pull factors.

The young woman is pushed away from her mother by hatred toward her mother. This hatred has its source in her belief that her mother has failed to provide her with a penis or has punitively taken it away. Secondly, it is derived from her Oedipal jealousy.

Less constantly, it is augmented by feelings of deprivation of maternal love, particularly if she has had to compete for her mother's love with seemingly preferred brothers. Or if she projects her own hostile feelings, she will feel unloved. Hatred can be augmented as well if a young woman experiences her mother as smothering, domineering, and controlling.

Reasons for her hatred, therefore, surely abound; and they combine to push her away from her mother.

The young woman is pulled toward her father by her need to undo the intense feelings of inferiority produced by her sense of castration.

In choosing her father as a love object and later a husband or lover she seeks to overcome her castration complex.

When a woman possesses a man, she also feels that she possesses and shares his penis. In lovemaking she literally incorporates his penis, and temporarily makes it her own.

She is also able to identify with her beloved and vicariously to share his phallus, his active masculine role, his masculinity and strength, and his aggressive ambitions and accomplishments.

By means of transient total identification, with a temporary loss of personal identity, she can fulfill her desire for union and oneness with her lover.

Masculine penetration represents a wish for union and oneness with a woman, and a desire to return to the womb. Or, as Otto Rank would say, it represents a desire to overcome the trauma of birth. A woman can by identification, therefore, also experience a vicarious return to the womb, when her partner enters her body. She can also achieve the same result by identifying with her unborn child.

Lovers of both sexes call each other "baby," attesting to the unconscious equation of a penis and child. For a woman the mere possession of "her man," "her baby," partially fulfills her wish for a child and a phallus, which is augmented, of course, when she bears him a child.

Having a child and a man also fulfills, of course, the young woman's influential and vital wish to identify with her mother, by having a husband and becoming a mother herself, in accordance with the Oedipal pattern. This is Oedipal victory! In a parallel manner, men can only achieve Oedipal victory by means of their love for a woman and their identification with their father, by means of becoming fathers themselves.

In men, calling a beloved baby implies that his love object represents a child that he can love in both a maternal and paternal fashion, or, by a process of identification, a beloved can represent his own self as a child that he can then narcissistically love.

It must be emphasized that the transition of a woman's love for her mother to her father obviously takes place, but matters are far from being that simple. Because it is not a question of either\or. A woman is quite capable of identifying her male love object with her mother, as well as with her father. The same process, in reverse, mutatis mutandis, occurs in men.

This is shown by the analysis of the meaning of over determined sexual practices that reveal that both sexes can and do use each other to gratify repressed <u>homosexual</u> wishes. Identifying with one's partner; and therefore vicariously enjoying active-masculine and passive-feminine roles, as well as interchanging child-parent roles basically accomplish this.

Fellatio, for example, involves an unconscious penis-breast equation, which therefore provides for a regressive nursing at the breast, as well as a symbolic, oral incorporation of the penis. It illustrates the manner in which a woman may fulfill a homosexual wish with a man. But, it also reveals how a man may fulfill his homosexual desires with a woman: by means of identifying with her. Therefore, heterosexual life, as odd as it may at first sight seem, allows the simultaneous satisfaction of male and female homosexual wishes, and wishes to play both the child and parental role.

All sexual activity is potentially bisexual activity. It is highly plausible that these potentialities enable both sexes to discharge latent homosexual feelings in a heterosexual context; so that they need not become intense enough to cause serious conflict and pathology.

In summary then, there are diverse and many attractions toward the father, which essentially provide a means of undoing and overcoming feelings of castration, inferiority, and Oedipal defeat. This does not imply a depreciation of the many other important wish fulfillments, mentioned above, that are provided by this momentous transition.

———————

It is to be noted that Freud's final formulation does not contain an explanation of the origin of castration anxiety or Oedipal guilt. This was because Freud maintained that these integral aspects of the complex had their origin in phylogenetic events, and that they were, therefore, historical acquisitions.

However, the origin of castration anxiety and Oedipal guilt can also be explained on ontogenetic lines.

To begin with, castration anxiety can be understood to reflect the child's own cruel, hostile, castrating wishes before the development of a moral conscience. It would then be the result of the child's wishes projected on to the parent of the opposite sex. Castration anxiety could then be understood to be a retaliatory fear.

Secondly, it can be understood as a derivative of the primitive logic prevailing in infancy during the phallic phase.

The child derives pleasure from infantile masturbation and the accompanying discharge of Oedipal fantasies. The reality and intensity of the pleasure experienced makes it seem as if the wishes have been fulfilled in reality.

A little boy then incorrectly conceives of castration as a punishment for Oedipal wishes because he holds his penis to be the responsible cause of his pleasurable sensations and his sexual wishes. He mistakenly perceives his penis to be the origin or source of both his pleasure and his Oedipal wishes. This implies a primitive confusion of cause (the sexual instinct) and effect (sexual discharge). A confusion between instinctual stimulus and masturbation response.

It is therefore understandable that he would imagine castration as an appropriate and fitting punishment for his Oedipal wishes, since it would result in the loss of the offending cause: an instrument idealized and highly valued as a source of pleasure.

However, the universality of this fear, cannot be accounted for without another factor described by Freud.

Castration anxiety is a product of the anatomical differences between the sexes and one of its psychological consequences. This is a result of the finding that the male child misinterprets his perception of the female genital to mean that castration is possible. Since he perceives the female genital organ as an absence of a phallus, he concludes that females have been castrated. This erroneous interpretation of sexual differences is remarkably shared by both sexes. The recognition of the anatomical difference between the sexes, accordingly, serves as a reinforcement and confirmation of the reality of castration.

A further psychological consequence of this misunderstanding is a fear and subsequent defensive devaluation of the female genital. Hostility to women is often the result of a defense against <u>fear</u> of women; fear that originates in the aforementioned source. It also originates in the related fear of the "castra<u>ting</u>" woman, one of the derivatives of female penis envy.

In both sexes, the female genital organ is devaluated as a "wound," menstruation is called "the curse"; and the depreciation is expressed faithfully, again in profane language, by calling the vulva a "cunt."

The legendary head of Medusa, the sight of which turns men into stone, illustrates the fear. This image can be explained as a frightening symbol of the "castrated" female genitalia. It inspires dread, in spite of the phallic symbolic overlay of the snakes.

Men are thus left with two contradictory attitudes to the female genital: instinctual attraction and almost unconscious repulsion. Women make a felicitous adaptation by the displacement of their vanity to their bodies as a whole; while retaining a strong need to keep their "pudenda" concealed, behind the seventh veil. This displacement is responsible for the billion-dollar beauty industry: cosmetics, perfumes, hair care, skin care, fashion clothes, jewelry, plastic surgery, exercise fads, weight reducing diets, and beauty magazines.
On the one hand, men in love "overestimate" the woman that they love to a ridiculous degree, and, on the other hand, they devaluate women to the same ridiculous degree. Reality probably lies somewhere between these two absurd extremes. But, then again, what has reality got to do with it?

These factors would, I believe, adequately explain the prevalence and universality of castration anxiety in terms of individual psychology and psychodynamics.

Oedipal guilt can also be explained on the basis of individual psychology. It can be derived from ambivalent feelings toward the parent of the same sex. The combination of love and hate toward the same person is the underlying basis for guilt.

One cannot hate a person that one loves without regret, remorse and guilt. The little boy, for example, would not feel guilty about wanting to harm his rival father if he did not also love, depend on, and identify with him. This affection has a homosexual component and is also related to the perception of the father as an idealized protector. It is because he admires and idealizes his father that he takes him as a model for identification. We tend to forget that children live with giants in the land of Brobdingnag.

There is another factor operative here that is surprisingly seldom expressed. This is the fact that children know that their parents are responsible in some way for giving them the gift of life. There is, therefore, a seldom-voiced sense of gratitude toward parents for life itself, unverbalized perhaps because it is taken for granted. This also helps to understand Oedipal guilt because hostility toward parents would involve ingratitude toward someone that one has to thank for life and parental care during a long period of dependency.

Be this as it may, a phylogenetic contribution cannot be excluded in the genesis of castration anxiety and Oedipal guilt. The fact that we are ignorant of the method of transmission of memories across the generations, does not logically prove or disprove that this communication did not take place, or that an archaic inheritance of prehistoric events in the human family does not exist.

VIII . METAPSYCHOLOGICAL REFLECTIONS

The psychological behavior of the individual can be traced back ultimately to biological needs. The science of psychology is based on the science of biology.

This does not mean, of course, that only biological forces decide human behavior. Since an individual grows and develops within a family setting, the relationships within a family also influence human behavior. Since a family is a unit of a larger society, social forces also impinge on the individual. Psychology and sociology are mutually complementary and necessary for the understanding of human behavior.

If one attempts to explain psychological behavior by going <u>beyond</u> biology, one enters a domain of speculation, supposition, and conjecture. In seeking explanations for psychological phenomena on a phylogenetic level, i.e., explanations related to the historical evolution of the human race, one treads on thin ice. One enters an area where one cannot prove or disprove a hypothesis.

Philosophical speculation, nonetheless, has its uses and value. Among other things it clarifies issues, although it may not provide definitive answers. It can often point the way to further knowledge.

In this regard, Freud's phylogenetic theory of the origin of the Oedipus complex is very useful in attempting to understand <u>the significance</u> of the complex. Besides, it is intellectually intriguing.

———————

We know very little about the type of social organization that prevailed in the earliest stages of mankind. Cultural anthropologists have abandoned idle speculations about a hypothetical "barbarous" state. However, ethology does throw some light on this subject; because there is no reason to believe that early human relationships were any different from those currently seen in our nearest evolutionary neighbors, the Simian anthropoid apes.

What is surprising is that there is a large diversity of sexual behavior among the anthropoid apes; a diversity that varies in proportion to the social structures in which sexual relations and child rearing occur.

The sexual ties among Simian apes, as a rule, depend on domination practices that prevail according to species. That is, the domination of one male over a clan, like what one finds in the Gorilla, or the complex hierarchies with a collective domination by various associated males.

One can see a variety of behavior ranging from the monogamy of the Gibbon apes to the regular promiscuity characteristic of the Chimpanzees.

The prohibition against incest exists among certain primates, as well as precise sexual prohibitions related to domination. Sexual competition for females is prevalent, and elaborate courtship rituals accompany it.

One can conclude that the same widespread variability existed among early human groups. There was then an evolution from social groups in which women were freely interchanged to the prevalence of monogamy.[47]

According to Claude Levi-Strauss, ever since historic times, all societies have had a social structure consisting of the monogamic family. The preeminence of the monogamic family is true for even the most primitive cultures extant today.[48]

Marriage in the original monogamic family was informal, and later formalized and given social approval. The social institution of marriage was essentially created to eliminate sexual competition for women who married, sexual competition that we have seen exists in the animal kingdom also. Although this may have been the original and still current purpose of marriage, it subsequently acquired many other purposes, e.g., the division of labor between the sexes, and the provision of lineage and property inheritance laws.

The monogamic conjugal family consisting of a more or less durable union, which was socially approved, of a man and a woman and their children is a universal phenomenon in every type of known society, everywhere.

By limiting sexual competition to the unmarried, the formation of an enduring family became possible. The institution of marriage implies the provision of exclusive sexual rights to the conjugal pair, which serves to avoid further sexual competition. The birth of the human family, therefore, is founded on monogamic marriage.

The formation of the monogamic, conjugal family not only provided for sexual rights; but also provided most importantly for the prohibition of sexual relations within the family.

In all societies, there is a universal prohibition of incest. At all times and in all places. The exceptions prove the rule. In Egypt, for example, incest was strictly limited to the high nobility, who thought of themselves as Gods, not mere mortals.

Because of the prohibition of incest, the requirement for the creation of a family is the existence of two families whose offspring can intermarry and create other families, which over the generations would create a mixed society. The interdiction of incest allows for the escape from incest by directing family members outside of their own family. There is, therefore, a mutual dependency between families, compelling them to produce new families in order to perpetuate themselves, and to recognize ties that are not consanguineous.

Social organization, accordingly, had its beginning in the incest-prohibition.

It must be emphasized that the incest prohibition changed the biological setting in which mating and procreation took place, namely, to the monogamic conjugal family. But, most consequentially, it changed the biological setting in which children grew and developed.

Within the monogamic family, children were reared in an intimate, enduring triangular setting with affectionate relationships. For the first time.

On the other hand, in the animal kingdom and in early human groups, mothers are devoted to their offspring, but this is not at all true for the fathers, who are out fishing [sic], hunting, and killing each other. The family as a triangular unit was a new and pivotal progressive step.

If we now turn to the conditions prevailing in the animal kingdom, one can see that by comparison no rules or regulations for mating and procreation exist. This therefore suggests that the incest interdiction was responsible for the evolution and passage of prehistoric man from animal life to human life and from nature to culture.

In the animal kingdom, there is no true society. The human animal became a human when he became a member of society.
Claude Levi-Strauss quoting Taylor says that the ultimate explanation for social organization "is probably that mankind has understood very early that, in order to free itself from a wild struggle for existence, it was confronted with the very simple choice of "either marrying-out or being killed out."[49]

However, it must be emphasized that the incest prohibition within society could prevent incest in society, but it could not prevent the occurrence of incestuous desires within a family.

This required a new process or evolution. It required a decisive change from an external interdiction to an internal control within the individual.

The new biological conditions within the monogamic, conjugal family and their psychological consequences accounts for this pivotal, decisive shift of social prohibition of incest to internal anxiety in the individual.

We already know what the biological requirements for this change were: the growth and development of the child in a triangular family setting, the prolonged dependency of the human child on its parents, and the flowering of sexuality in infancy.

The psychological consequences of these biological givens in the monogamic, conjugal family were: our old friend the Oedipus complex. Indeed!

The Oedipus complex produced the required castration anxiety needed to provide an <u>inner</u> incest barrier.

The details of this psychological development within the child have already been provided in the preceding description of Freud's ontogenetic theory, and need not be repeated.

Since the development of the incest prohibition serves to explain so much, one is led to wonder what explains the origin of the incest prohibition?

The answer is unknown.

However, the analysis and interpretation of Totemism offers some idea about conditions that caused this development. Freud's excellent reconstruction of possible events has been described earlier in this essay, in the chapter devoted to the phylogenetic theory.

It can now be understood why his formulation of the phylogenetic theory is so valuable; since it provides a possible explanation of the origin of the incest prohibition.

———————

There are many implications of this novel perspective.

To begin with, it implies that ritual forms of prohibition were no longer required after incest dread was relocated inside the individual. This accounts for the fact that these social rituals gradually died out; but, of course, rules of marriage, kinship, religious, and legal laws that prohibit incest remain.

Regardless, memories of what had occurred in the prehistoric period before the incest-prohibition persisted without the rituals. This took the form of myths, legends, and later dramas about the past. The Oedipus play is a case in point; since it was based on legends transmitted by oral tradition: by storytellers, soothsayers, oracles, and priests in ancient Greece. Other residues, traces, and vestiges of the ancient prehistoric events remain in the form of such religious rituals as the Jewish custom of circumcision, a symbolic castration. And, the Catholic belief in Original Sin, i.e., the Oedipal crimes of our forefathers.

From generation to generation, from century to century, the prehistoric events that preceded the development of the Oedipus complex were transmitted in society by myths, legends, and religious practices and ceremonies.

This is neither a mystery nor a problem. It is perfectly comprehensible.

However, there was no transmission of memories across the generations by means of some unknown hereditary, genetic, gonadic mechanism, some mysterious phylogenetic memory, some archaic inheritance, some vague constitutional predisposition, some collective unconscious process, and some Lamarckian inheritance of acquired characteristics.

This was neither necessary nor required. There is no reason to believe that such a genetic transmission or communication exists.

This is because the normal growth and development of the Oedipus complex in the child effectively perpetuated, in each succeeding generation, an inner taboo against incest by the development in all human beings of castration anxiety. Castration anxiety conceived as a punishment for Oedipal wishes.

It is important to notice a curious, corroborating fact that is usually taken for granted and overlooked. This is the fact that children are not explicitly taught that incest is forbidden. The topic or even the word is never mentioned. The reason is precisely because it is unnecessary to forbid incest. All children learn that incest is forbidden by the development of their own Oedipus complex. The unconscious process is quite sufficient and efficient in delivering this lesson. Adults, who have learned this lesson unconsciously in childhood avoid incest. Not because of legal laws against it in society, but because of a defense against castration anxiety.

———

As evidence for the existence of a phylogenetic memory, Freud pointed out that typical symptoms, typical dreams, and typical fantasies cannot be traced back or explained by events in the past life of the individual. What is most important, he also pointed out that the Oedipus complex itself could not be traced back to events in the past life of the individual, nor could it be related to a special situation in the past.

Freud perhaps saw the complex as something basically pathological; because he discovered it during his studies of the neuroses, and because he spent his treatment time trying to overcome its ill effects. His clinical orientation, therefore, unduly influenced his conception of the complex.

The reason the Oedipus complex cannot be traced back to a special or unusual situation in the past is that it is a normal developmental process. It is not a product of psychopathology. It does not require special or extraordinary causes for its development or explanation. The biological conditions and their psychological consequences, previously defined, are more than adequate to explain its happening and its universality.

———————

The development of the Oedipus complex is not only inevitable but also eminently <u>necessary</u>.

As a result of its presence, family life is made possible. If it were absent, there would be a return to the same internecine strife that existed in prehistoric times.

Typical symptoms, dreams, and fantasies <u>are</u> related to identical, typical experiences that are common to different individuals. The underlying basis and explanation of these typical, recurring phenomena is the central, collective, and universal experience in everyone's childhood: the normal development of the Oedipus complex.

The archetypal experiences that are common to different individuals, the common denominator of these experiences, are quite simply: <u>growing up in a family</u>.

In the final analysis, the causal basis of the Oedipus complex can be reduced to two words: <u>sexual jealousy</u>.

The emotion of jealousy arises in the context of <u>competition</u> for a sexual love object. It implies an unwillingness and inability to share a love object with another person. The unwillingness to share is founded on the child's limitless and insatiable narcissism. Jealousy accordingly has two components. A desire for the exclusive possession of a love object. And, secondly, the potential for hostility toward both a disloyal partner and toward any rival. The basis of jealousy can be traced, therefore, to egoism and vanity. The egoistic element is obvious and the narcissistic element can be easily deduced.

However, the narcissistic component becomes apparent when jealous rage is traced to the fact that sexual disloyalty is interpreted as invidiously implying inferiority in the jealous person when compared to his rival.

The well-known jealous Latin lover and the tradition of "machismo" illustrate this in Latin America. Latin lovers are very sensitive to the slightest suggestion of unfaithfulness in their female partners. Disloyalty is typically imaginary and unrealistic. This sensitivity is based on an insecurity about their own masculinity; which is, accordingly, exaggerated by reaction formations to their inner sense of inferiority. The sensitivity can, perhaps, be traced back to the easily observed fact that Latin parents have a very intense, indulgent loving relationship with their children. And, with the fact that women have a very devalued place in Latin culture.

Sexual infidelity, real or imaginary, is interpreted as a narcissistic affront on the betrayed lover's fragile masculinity and evokes proportionate rage and a desire for revenge. Stories of revenge are very popular in Latin American cultures. It is this factor that helps to account for the excessive jealous rage found in triangular situations.

The sexual jealousy of the child is understandable but irrational; because it is based on a narcissistic inability to share a sexual love object, and a wish for exclusive possession that is inherently impossible.

As mentioned previously, all the wishes of the Oedipus complex in childhood are incapable of fulfillment and doomed to failure and disappointment. Jealousy produces the rivalry with the parent of the same sex. But, it is a rivalry between very unequal contestants. For the child a no-win situation. It is perhaps for these reasons that the Oedipus complex of the child has a sad and tragic quality. And, therefore it was only a classic Greek tragedy that was a highly suitable vehicle for its expression.

On the other hand, jealousy between adults can be a normal and realistic emotion. It becomes abnormal if unconscious wishes to be unfaithful are projected onto one's partner. The formula then is:" I am not disloyal to you, but you are disloyal to me." Jealousy becomes delusional when homosexual wishes are projected. A woman, for example, will then imagine and insist that her husband or lover is sexually interested in those women toward whom she herself has an unconscious attraction.

A phylogenetic theory is not required to explain the Oedipus complex. It can be adequately explained on a pure ontogenetic basis, as was outlined above in Freud's final synthesis.

But, on the other hand, (said Tevye to the fiddler on the roof) the theory does illuminate the profound meaning and significance of the complex.

From this innovative perspective, it can now be understood clearly that there is no need to "overcome" or "destroy" the Oedipus complex. There is no "destruction" of the complex; only a repression and passing of the complex in the course of development.

Neurosis, on the other hand, can be understood, from this vantage point, to represent a development of the Oedipus complex that has gone astray. Neurosis is the Oedipus complex gone haywire!

Neurotic phenomena, in contrast to the complex itself, can be traced back to unusual and special events in the past that led to an intensification of normal Oedipal conflicts. Examples of important adventitious events of this type have already been provided.

Primarily because of the intensification of certain conflicts, the self is required to resolve them irrationally by means of primitive mental processes. It is the excessive unconscious conflicts that must be overcome and not the Oedipus complex itself. The excessive degree of conflict is what disturbs the equilibrium of the self and tips the scales in favor of illness. Besides, the elimination of the Oedipus complex is hardly either desirable or even possible. One cannot eliminate human sexual jealousy.

Although castration anxiety is an unrealistic imaginary fear, and although Oedipal guilt is not based on real crimes; they are never eliminated. Oedipal defeat persists as an illusion with its attendant inferiority feelings. Incestuous and parricidal wishes never perish either. It may be unrealistic and unwise to feel guilty about mere wishes; but we certainly do. Ambivalent feelings of love and hate that are almost equal in degree and intensity can be changed, so that one or the other predominates in a post ambivalent state; but neither one nor the other is completely eradicated.

No mortal being is rational enough or sane enough to "destroy" these elements of the Oedipus complex. Yes, of course, their excessive presence can be diminished and mastered in the name of reason and sanity; but not erased altogether.

One would like ideally to control and master our unruly sexuality as well; as in the well-known metaphor of the rider on a horse, but, as Freud quipped: "Wir sind nur Sonntags Reiter."

In a world of science fiction, on another planet, a being that could be imagined without an Oedipus complex would not be a human being. He would simply be a human animal, just as he once was in the past.

Through an obscure process of social evolution, the Oedipus complex became part of our <u>human nature</u> and heritage. It is now part of our being.

The Oedipus complex can be: repressed, forgotten, and denied. The feelings that it contains can be attenuated and transferred, and they can be modified by multiple defense mechanisms.

It can be: relived, acted out, and reconstructed.

The Oedipus complex cannot be remembered.

It cannot be <u>destroyed</u>!

Freud originally presented the Oedipus complex as a discovery concerning the unconscious mental life of the child. It essentially was conceived as a discovery of what takes place in a triangular relationship between mother, father, and child. It revealed that this triangular relationship manifested a competition between the child and the parent of the same sex. This inevitably engendered feelings of rivalry, jealousy, incest, and parricide. It revealed the egoistic and narcissistic core in every child.

This constellation was seen as a discovery of what takes place in the mind of the child. However, it was subsequently realized that the father and mother are part of the triangle and, of course, they play a role. The Oedipus complex of the child will differ according to the personalities of the parents, their relationship with each other, and their particular preferences among their own children. The parents also have incestuous wishes towards their children and hostile wishes towards their respective spouses. Therefore, from the point of view of the members of the triangle taken as a whole, the Oedipus complex can equally well be called the Family Complex or Triangle Complex, since it revealed unconscious feelings of the same nature in the mother and father. So, one can argue that Freud not only discovered an important truth about a child's feelings toward his parents, but he also discovered an important truth about the nature of the unconscious feelings that exist in every <u>family.</u>

<u>Finally,</u> we are led to recognize that it was not an important truth about the child or even about the family that he discovered. Rather, it was an important truth about human nature in general. This is because all human beings operate in a context of competition, and, as a result, we all possess all the feelings described with the term Oedipus complex. Oedipus is simply everyone!

Since this is true, the discovery of the Oedipus complex was a contribution to the understanding of essential unconscious features of human nature. Therefore, it cannot be dispensed with as an old outdated theory, to be supplanted by the latest fad in psychoanalytic theory.

IX. CLOSING REMARKS

We have retraced Freud's footsteps from the time of his initial discovery of the Oedipus complex in 1897 to his final formulation shortly before his death in 1939. The preceding chronological reconstruction, has, I believe, fulfilled the promise of a consistent, coherent, and cogent theory.

Freud liked to think of himself as a Conquistador because, like Cortes, he explored and conquered unexplored territory. The new territory was the maze of the unconscious mind and the hieroglyphic forms and transformations of infantile sexuality.

Sigmund Freud was many things besides a Conquistador. Obviously a psychological genius. A scientist of the first rank. An anthropologist and archeologist of the primitive human mind. A philosopher to be sure. A writer with literary talent. The Sherlock Holmes of the psychopathology of everyday life. And an archeologist manqué. Finally, as Nietzsche would say, he was menschlich alzo menschlich, and perhaps for this reason the most admirable.

I have merely tried to provide a thread of Ariadne to lead us through the maze of his oeuvre, so that we could follow his footsteps into the light of knowledge.

The preceding account of his work covers a period of over four decades. The idea of the Oedipus complex is interwoven into the entire fabric of his work. I have extracted only certain threads from a very rich tapestry. Therefore, I could not portray the richness, the detail, the style, or the subtlety of his thinking on this topic.

Perhaps I have made the forest visible, in spite of the trees.

All clinical applications aside, the idea of the Oedipus complex is unique in the history of ideas. This is because I am not aware of any other important scientific discovery that required self-analysis. This required a great man and not only a great scientist for its accomplishment.

Charles Darwin was a great scientist, but I do not think that he is considered a great man. The idea of human evolution did not originate with Darwin. What he accomplished was the development of the idea and the provision of overwhelming proof of our human descent from our animal neighbors. His ideas also offended the narcissism of the society that he lived in. His society preferred to believe in the illusion that God created us, rather than in our evolution from the lowly anthropoid apes. (Darwin himself was an agnostic, or so he claims.)

In a similar fashion, the idea of the Oedipus complex would have to be attributed technically to Diderot. However, it was Freud, like Darwin, who developed and proved the idea, and offended the vanity of the ungrateful society in which he lived.

There have been, of course, innumerable worthwhile contributions to the literature of the Oedipus complex by many other analysts after Freud, notably by Melanie Klein. However, to include them here would have been to write another book.

I attempted to inject a note of dry humor here and there in this study to lighten a work that deals with a very "heavy" theme indeed.

I think (at least I hope) Freud would forgive me for the poetic license that I occasionally used in the preceding Talmudic exegesis of his work; since I followed the spirit of his work, but not the letter of his grand endeavor to explore the unknown.

The reader can now see that Oedipus Rex, the tragic king, is alive and well, and that he is living in all of us, all over, all over, the world!

FIN

References

All references in the text to the writings of Sigmund Freud listed below refer to: The Standard Edition of the Complete Psychological Works of Sigmund Freud (James Strachey , ed., Hogarth Press. London).

1.Freud, S .(1940) An Outline of Psychoanalysis,Vol. 23, p.141.

2.(1950) The Origins of Psychoanalysis, Letter 64, Vol. 1, p.207.

3. ibid, , letter 71, p.221.

4. (1950) The Interpretation of Dreams ,Vol .4, p.247.

5.(1950) The Origins of Psychoanalysis, Vol. 1, p.223.

6.(1896) Heredity and the Etiology of the Neuroses, Vol. 3, p.143.
   The Etiology of Hysteria, Vol .3 p.189

7.(1894) Neuropsychoses of Defense, Vol. 3, p. 43.

8.(1950) The Origins of Psychoanalysis. Vol. 1, p. 68.)
 (1898) Sexuality in the Etiology of the Neuroses, Vol. 3, p, 263.

9.(1950) Three Essays on the Theory of Sexuality, Vol. 7, p. 126..

10.(1909) Notes on a Case of Obsessional Neurosis, Vol. 10, P.157.

11.(1899) Screen Memories, VOL. 3, p. 206.

12,(1909) Analysis of a Phobia in a Five-Year-Old Boy, Vol. 12. p.329.

13.(1913) Five Lectures on Psychoanalysis, Vol. 12, P.206.

14.(1905) Three Essays on the Theory of Sexuality, Vol. 7, P.126.

15.(1914) On narcissism, An Introduction, Vol. 14, p.69.

16.(1912) The Dynamics of the Transference, Vol. 12, p.98.

17.(1919) A Child is Being Beaten, Vol. 17, p.177.

18.(1924) The Dissolution of the Oedipus Complex, Vol. 19, p.172.

19.(1912) Totem and Taboo, Vol. 13, p.5.

20.(1923)The Ego and the Id, Vol. 19, p.4.

21.(1912) The Dynamics of the Transference, Vol. 12, p.98.

22.(1914) Some Reflections On Schoolboy Psychology, Vol.,13, p.240.

23. (1913) On Psychoanalysis, Vol. 12. p.206.

24. Ibíd. ,p.210.

25. (1912) Types of Onset of Neurosis, Vol. 12, p.207.

26. (1916) A general Introduction to Psychoanalysis, Vol, 15, p.3.

27.(1912) Contribution to the Psychology of Love, Vol. 11, p.178.

28. Ibid, p.203.

29.(1919) A Child is Being Beaten, Vol. 17, p.190.

30.(1921) Group Psychology and the Analysis of the Ego, Vol. 18, p.67.

31.(1920) the Psychogenesis of Case of Homosexuality in a Woman, Vol. 18, p.146.

32.(1911) psychoanalytic Notes Upon an Autobiographical Account of Paranoia, Vol. 12,p.3

33.(1912) The Dynamics of the Transference Vol.12, p.98.

34.(1918)From the History of an Infantile Neurosis, Vol. 19, p.71.

35.(1913) A general Introduction to Psychoanalysis, Vol. 12, p.206.

36.(1918) From the History of an Infantile Neurosis. Vol. 19, p.69.

37. Ibid. p.70.

38.(1912) Totem and Taboo, Vol. 13, p.8.

39.(1923) The Ego and the Id, Vol. 19, p.40.

40. ibid.p.42

41.(1901) An Autobiographical Note, Vol. 3, p.24.

42.(1923) The Infantile Genital Organization of the Libido Vol. 19, p.143.

43.(1923)The Ego and the Id, Vol. 19, p.41.

44.(1931 Female Sexuality, Vol. 7, p .309.

45. (1925) Some Psychological Consequences of the Psychological Differences Between the Sexes, Vol. 22, p.7.

46.(1931) Female Sexuality, Vol. 7, p.308.

47.Chopin, Marie-Joseph, LA VIDA SEXUAL, Publicaciones Cruz O., Mexico, 1993,p.18.

48.Levi-Strauss, Claude," The Family," in ANTHROPOLOGY, Edited by Samuel Rapport and Helen Wright, New York, 1968,p.142.

49.Ibid. p.162.

CPSIA information can be obtained at www.ICGtesting.com
Printed in the USA
BVOW03s0347200314

348123BV00003B/890/A